BENTLEY

A MOTORING
MISCELLANY

—

A
RANDOM REFERENCE
FOR THE
MODERN ENTHUSIAST

NICHOLAS FOULKES

Compilation copyright © 2005
Nicholas Foulkes
Illustrations copyright © 2005
Mark Watkinson
(pages 27, 40, 60–2, 90–5, 125, 136)

Editorial Director JANE O'SHEA
Project Editor LISA PENDREIGH
Editorial Assistant LAURA HERRING
Creative Director HELEN LEWIS
Art Director & Designer LAWRENCE MORTON
Illustrator MARK WATKINSON
Production Director VINCENT SMITH
Production Controller RUTH DEARY

Pages 14–15 reprinted by permission
of Bentley. Page 16 reprinted by
permission of Christie's. Page 20
reprinted by permission of Bentley.
Page 21 from *Exceptional Motor Cars from
the Collection of Sir Elton John, CBE*,
Christie's International Motor Cars
Ltd, 2001, reprinted by permission
of Christie's. Page 24 from *W.O.* by
W.O. Bentley, Hutchinson, 1958.
Page 35 from *The Savoy Cocktail Book* by
Harry Craddock, Pavilion, 2003,
reprinted by permission of The Savoy,
a Fairmont hotel and Pavilion Books,
a division of Chrysalis. Pages 38–39
from *Casino Royale, Moonraker, Thunderball*
and *On Her Majesty's Secret Service* by
Ian Fleming, reprinted by permission
of Glidrose Productions Ltd/Ian
Fleming Publications. Page 44 from
Bentley Factory Cars 1919–1931 by Michael
Hay, Osprey Books. Page 49 reprinted
by permission of Bentley. Pages 50–51
from *Those Bentley Days* by A.F.C.
Hilstead, Faber, 1953. Page 52
reprinted by permission of Bentley.
Page 109–12 reprinted by permission
of Bentley.

First published in 2005 by Quadrille
Publishing Limited
Alhambra House, 27–31 Charing
Cross Road, London WC2H 0LS

The rights of Nicholas Foulkes have
been asserted by the Copyright,
Design and Patent Act 1988.

Cataloguing in Publication Data: a
catalogue record for this book is
available from the British Library.

ISBN 1-84400-240-3

Printed and bound in China.

DEDICATION

For all those who, like me,
have pursued their passion for
the winged B even unto
financial disaster.

CONTENTS

CONTENTS

CONTENTS

INTRODUCTION

This book is not intended to replace or update any of the existing books about Bentley Motors, instead it is a magpie-like assembly of curiosities concerning this evocative British automotive marque: a smorgasbord of esoteric information to be devoured at one sitting or picked at over time. Do not look for a narrative, nor even a hint of chronological development – you will not find either. It does not pretend to be a complete survey of the Bentley marque in any way, however, if you want to find out more about W.O. Bentley's life as an early twentieth-century biker or if you ever idly wondered how much Sir Elton John's Bentleys fetched at auction then there is something to amuse you in the following pages, where everything from coachbuilders to torque curves, from Bentley cocktails to W.O.'s role in the downfall of the Red Baron plays a part.

LIST OF TOASTS AT THE FIRST
ANNUAL DINNER OF BENTLEY MOTORS LTD,
(SERVICE DEPARTMENT)

Hotel Great Central, Marylebone W
Friday December 3rd, 1926

The King
PROPOSED BY
CAPT. WOOLF BARNATO

❦

The Firm
PROPOSED BY
DR J.D. BENJAFIELD

REPLY
RAMSAY MANNERS ESQ

❦

The Directors
PROPOSED BY
H. KENSINGTON MOIR ESQ

REPLY
CAPT. WOOLF BARNATO

❦

The Visitors
PROPOSED BY
W.K. FORSTER ESQ

REPLY
IVOR McLURE ESQ

❦

The Chairman
PROPOSED BY
H. PIKE ESQ

A GRAND PRIX DE DANSE
will be held at
ARDENRUN, near LINGFIELD
On Saturday, June 29th, 1929

THIS event takes place over a course consisting of supper, dancing, and fair drinking, commencing at 10 p.m. on Saturday until 6 a.m. on Sunday. Any competitors still drinking or dancing after that hour will be flagged off the course!

The course is a natural one, and of course the only course open to you is naturally to enter as a matter of course, (How coarse!!!)

An entry form is enclosed for you and a passenger.

No ballast need be carried if you desire to run solo.

AWARDS

1ST PRIZE: A ride down the drive in No. 1 "Bentley" to the prettiest girl. Driver: Barnato or Birkin — au choix

2ND PRIZE: Same ride in No. 9 "Bentley." Driver: Kidston or Dunfee — au choix

3RD (OR CONSOLATION) PRIZE: Same ride. Driver: Benjafield

SAFETY REGULATIONS

1 Crash helmets must be worn in the event of winning first prize.

2 Roller skates must be carried, but need not be worn, in the event of winning second prize.

3 Safety belts and police whistles must be worn in event of winning consolation prize.

THE HIGHEST PRICE EVER ACHIEVED BY A BENTLEY AT AUCTION

O N 23RD JULY, 2004, a 1930 Speed Six — bodied by Vanden Plas, ex-works, No. 2 Team Car, winner of the Double Twelve race and 2nd at Le Mans 1930 — was sold at Christie's Le Mans Classic auction in France for **Eu 4,188,250** (£2,784,741) to an unnamed private buyer.

BENTLEY CONTINENTAL GT PAINT COLOURS AND FINISHES

COLOUR	BENTLEY NAME	TYPE
Black	*Beluga*	Solid
	Diamond Black	Metallic
White	*Glacier White*	Solid
Blue	*Silverlake*	Metallic
	Neptune	Metallic
	Dark Sapphire	Metallic
Red	*St. James*	Solid
	Umbrian Red	Metallic
Green	*Midnight Emerald*	Metallic
	Barnato Green	Solid
	Spruce	Metallic
	Cypress	Metallic
Silver	*Moonbeam*	Metallic
	Silver Tempest	Metallic
Brown	*Chestnut*	Metallic
	Antique Gold	Metallic

SINCE 1998 the Bentley factory at Crewe has been transformed, with a major investment in advanced equipment and the very latest production technologies to assist the craftsmen and women. However, owners can be assured that each Bentley remains very much a hand-build creation. There are only two places on the production line where tasks are performed by robots and not human beings: the first being the lacquer spraying of the highly-polished fine wood veneers of the fascia, consoles and trim, and the second being the robotic application of a consistent bead of adhesive around the edge of a Bentley's windscreen prior to installation.

W.O. BENTLEY FACTS

HE WAS THE youngest of nine children.

AS A CHILD he disliked being called Walter (in later life he was known as W.O.).

ONE OF HIS most treasured childhood toys was a stationary steam engine, given to him by an uncle.

AT THE AGE of nine, he bought a second-hand bicycle and used to dismantle it with 'a frequency and thoroughness that terrified my mother.'

HIS FIRST EXPERIENCE of what he called 'independent travel over a long distance' came at age 14, when he cycled 130 miles to Wroxham, he covered the distance in a day.

HIS FIRST JOB was an apprenticeship with the Great Northern Railway

HIS FIRST JOB in the motor trade was with the National Motor Cab Company in Hammersmith.

HIS FIRST CAR was a chain-drive 9hp Riley

BEFORE WORD WAR I, he went into business with his brother selling a French car called DFP (Doriot, Flandrin et Parant).

WHEN ROLLS-ROYCE purchased Bentley, he worked for a while testing cars, before going to work at Lagonda.

WHILE HOLIDAYING IN the South of France in 1939, he heard the news that Hitler was about to invade Poland. Consequently, he drove to Dieppe, but due to overcrowding of the boats heading for Newhaven, he was forced to leave his Lagonda behind.

HE WAS AN enthusiastic follower of cricket and a keen photographer.

A LUNCH TO celebrate his eightieth birthday was held at the Esso Motor Hotel, Maidenhead, on September 21st, 1968.

"BENTLEY DRIVERS CLUB"

IF YOU ARE INTERESTED IN THE FORMATION OF
THE ABOVE-NAMED PROPOSED CLUB, WILL YOU
PLEASE COMMUNICATE WITH:

G. K. PELMORE,
H12, SLOANE AVENUE MANSIONS
CHELSEA, S.W.3.
'PHONE KENSINGTON 7020

MAKING ANY SUGGESTIONS YOU CAN, WHICH
MIGHT BE OF USE?

14TH MARCH 1936.

THE Bentley Drivers' Club was founded by Keston
Pelmore, who left cards on the windscreens of vintage
Bentleys parked at Brooklands race track in Weybridge,
Surrey, during the first meeting of 1936. Of that first meeting,
Keston Pelmore later wrote:

> On the date concerned there was an excellent attendance of no
> less than twenty-six people, and in fact by about 5 p.m. it was
> necessary to telephone the Boltons Hotel at 326, Earl's Court
> Road, and ask them if they could provide us with a larger room
> in which to continue the meeting.

In 2005, the membership stands at 3,555 in 22 countries.

PRICES REALISED BY BENTLEYS BELONGING TO SIR ELTON JOHN, CBE, AUCTIONED BY CHRISTIE'S, JUNE 5TH, 2001

1956 Bentley S1 Continental Fastback   £196,250
CHRISTIE'S TOP SELLING POST-WAR BENTLEY

1960 Bentley S2 Flying Spur   £67,550

1964 Bentley S3 Standard Steel Saloon   £54,050

1964 Bentley S3 Continental 'Chinese Eye'
Drophead Coupé   £69,750

1965 Bentley S3 Continental Coupé   £41,125

1975 Bentley Corniche   £49,350

1987 Bentley Turbo R Saloon   £49,350

1994 Bentley Continental   £163,250
(ONE OF THE LAST BUILT)

1997 Bentley Turbo R 400 Saloon   £82,950

SOME BENTLEY FACTORY TERMS

RAT-TRAP	A part of the braking system
SQUIRMING IRMA	A device used to test seat cushions on Bentleys and Rolls-Royces
PIGS	Distribution valves found in the Rat-Trap
MAE'S LEG	Underwing heat ducting in the S series
TEXAS DUCT	An air-con ducting fabricated in Texas
SPANISH HAT	Part of the bodyshell near the fuel filler area
WATERFALL CONSOLE	One of the consoles available in an Arnage
GOAT'S HEAD CONSOLE	Ditto
BIRD'S BEAK	A bit of trim for an on-board computer on the rear parcel shelf

W.O. BENTLEY AND THE RED BARON

DURING Word War I, W.O. Bentley designed engines for fighter aircraft: Bentley Rotary One (B.R.I) and Bentley Rotary Two (B.R.II). As part of his work, W.O. would take tours of the airfields. On one occasion he recalls being strafed by Germany's famous Baron Manfred von Richthofen; W.O. was forced to jump into a canal to save himself. Von Richthofen's second strafing run sent another man, Petty Officer Clarke, into the canal. The two men became friends and 'Nobby' Clarke would later become head racing mechanic of Bentley Motors.

Known as the Red Baron, von Richthofen downed eighty Allied aircraft, but he was finally shot down on April 22nd, 1918, during the second Battle of the Somme. The plane that shot him down was a Sopwith Camel, flown by Capt. A.R. Brown and powered by a Bentley Rotary Two. As he said later,

> I almost felt a pang of regret when Brown in a Camel, powered by one of our B.R.IIs, caught him at last.

THE FIRST CUSTOMER OF BENTLEY MOTORS

As W.O. BENTLEY put it in his 1958 biography, *W.O.*, Bentley Motors began life as a sort of invitation-only club, the price of membership being the cost of a Bentley. But money alone was not enough to secure one of those early Bentleys. W.O. was particularly concerned that his 'choice' (Bentley's word) of first owner sent out the right message:

> He would naturally be sympathetic to the sort of car we were producing or he wouldn't be paying over £1,000 for his model. But he also had to be something of a social butterfly who would mix in the best social strata and spread the good word far and wide, and something of an engineer who could appreciate the qualities of the car, talk about them authoritatively, and come back to explain any snags to us.

He wasn't asking for much. In the end, W.O. found just such a man. The first customer of a 3-litre production Bentley, bodied as a low coupé, was Noel van Raalte, described by Bentley as 'very rich', 'very sociable' and possessed of 'excellent mechanical knowledge'. As an undergraduate at Cambridge, van Raalte endeared himself to the college authorities and fellow road users by racing around the streets of the fenland university town in reverse gear in a Grand Prix Mercedes.

W.O.'s faith in van Raalte as a proselytizer of the marque was not misplaced. Van Raalte soon struck up a lively correspondence with the motoring press. 'The reason I bought a Bentley was because of its exceptional performance in all respects on the road,' wrote van Raalte on the correspondence page of *The Autocar* on October 1st, 1921. However this was but a prelude to the sort of encomium that eclipses even the firm's most grandiose advertisements of later years.

Such features as steering, suspension, holding the road, brakes, change speed, and engine efficiency, leave nothing to be desired, and are, in my opinion, to be found to a higher degree in this make of car than any other of the many makes I have owned or used. I dislike drawing comparison.

However, he did not dislike it enough to make a very telling one.

I admire the Rolls-Royce intensely, and have owned two of them, and must say that, as regards the features I have mentioned, the Bentley is far in advance of it, while the price is £750 less.

Given that it was only two years earlier that first Bentley engine had spluttered to life, one could be forgiven for thinking that van Raalte was a major shareholder, keen to see his investment pay off. However just in case the readers of *The Autocar* thought he was applying for the job of P.R. director of the newly founded Bentley motor company, he hastily added 'I have no interest in the company beyond owning and appreciating one of their cars.'

ALL BENTLEYS feature the flat winged B badge on the radiator. The winged B was designed for W.O. by the well-known motoring artist F. Gordon Crosby. Despite appearing symmetrical, the badge's wings have a different number of feathers on each side, intended to fool those who wish to copy the marque's famous logo.

The radiator badge has appeared in a variety of colours over the years. All cars up to 1924 appeared with red badges; thereafter green, blue and black appeared. During the late 1990s, the Arnage made its debut fitted with a twin-turbo BMW engine and a green badge. However, marque purists found that the BMW engine lacked the characteristic low-down torque and all-round 'Bentleyness' of its predecessor and so the 6.75 litre turbocharged Bentley engine went back under the bonnet of the Arnage. In order to distinguish it from its fellow Arnages, a red badge graced the radiator.

The tall winged B mascot was first used on a 1930 8 Litre, but was not generally fitted to Derby models. It was available as an option for an additional charge of five guineas.

Indeed, during the 1930s, it appears that consideration was given to scrapping this now iconic emblem. During 1935, a competition was held inviting readers of *The Autocar* to submit their own designs for a replacement mascot, with the winner to receive £50. However, it seems that many of those who entered the competition did not know the first thing about automotive design; many of the designs submitted by *The Autocar*'s armchair designers did not even allow for the bonnet to be opened.

On December 6th, 1935, it was announced that 'Nothing sufficiently outstanding was entered,' and that 'no design has been selected.' Two consolation prizes of £25 were awarded to C.J. Linzell and Maurice C. Taylor.

SOME NOTABLE BENTLEY OWNERS,
PAST AND PRESENT

TALLULAH BANKHEAD	
PRINCE BIRA OF SIAM	3½ Litre bodied by Vanden Plas; 4½ Litre Drophead bodied by James Young
JACK BUCHANAN	1931 8 Litre Saloon bodied by H.J. Mulliner
SIR MALCOLM CAMPBELL	4¼ Litre Tourer bodied by Vanden Plas and painted in Campbell Blue
RT HON ALAN CLARK MP	6½ Litre (his first car, purchased during his last term at Eton); R-Type Continental (nicknamed Bang Bang, recorded stolen during the 1950s, written off by joyriders and then rebodied by Bradley Brothers as a two-seater); Continental R; Continental S with West of England cloth upholstery and black stove-enamelled wheels
GARY COOPER	1956 S1 Continental bodied by Park Ward

SOME NOTABLE BENTLEY OWNERS, PAST AND PRESENT

PRINCESS ARTHUR OF CONNAUGHT	Derby Bentley
SIR BERNARD DOCKER	1957 S1 Continental bodied by H.J. Mulliner
LADY DOCKER	1956 S1 Continental Drophead Coupé bodied by Park Ward
CAPT. GEORGE EYSTON	Derby 3½ Litre
HM THE QUEEN	2002 State Limousine
HRH PRINCE GEORGE (LATER KING GEORGE V)	Speed Six bodied by Gurney Nutting; 4½ Litre Saloon bodied by Gurney Nutting
HRH PRINCE GEORGE (DUKE OF KENT)	4½ Litre; 6½ Litre; 8 Litre; Derby 3½ Litre; Derby 4¼ Litre
HRH THE PRINCE OF WALES (LATER KING EDWARD VIII)	4½ Litre Saloon bodied by Gurney Nutting with special golf club lockers, raised window sills, interior-operated spot lamps and semaphore indicators
HRH THE PRINCE OF WALES	Turbo RL
REX HARRISON	1959 S1 Continental bodied by Park Ward

KING HASSAN II OF MOROCCO	1961 S2 Continental Drophead Coupé bodied Park Ward
JOOLS HOLLAND, OBE	1958 S1 Continental
GERTRUDE LAWRENCE	
RALPH LAUREN	4½ Litre Supercharged
JAY LENO	1931 8 Litre four-door; Speed Six; 1924 3 Litre with 8-litre engine and twin-turbos; 4 Litre with 8-litre engine
SIR ALFRED MCALPINE	1954 R-Type Continental bodied by H.J. Mulliner; 1956 S1 Continental Drophead Coupé bodied by Park Ward
DUDLEY MOORE, CBE	1963 S3 Continental
STAVROS NIARCHOS	1953 R-Type Continental bodied by H.J. Mulliner
ARISTOTLE ONASSIS	1953 R-Type Continental bodied by H.J. Mulliner
KEITH RICHARDS	Bentley S Touring Continental (nicknamed Blue Lena)

SOME NOTABLE BENTLEY OWNERS, PAST AND PRESENT

BARONNE DE ROTHSCHILD	1958 S1 Continental Drophead Coupé bodied by Park Ward
PETER SELLERS	1959 S1 Continental, two-door with honeymoon express fins, bodied by Park Ward
THE SHAH OF IRAN	1955 R-Type Continental bodied by H.J. Mulliner
TERRY THOMAS	1959 S2 Continental Drophead Coupé bodied by Park Ward

Bentley Continentals of the 1950s and 1960s were all coachbuilt. Coachbuilders who worked on the Bentley R-Type, S-Type and S2 and S3 Continentals, and the number of cars they bodied, are listed below:

R-TYPE CONTINENTAL

H.J. Mulliner 193
Park Ward 6
Franay 5
Graber 3
Pininfarina 1

S2 CONTINENTAL[†]

H.J. Mulliner 222
Park Ward 125
James Young 40
Hooper 1

S1 CONTINENTAL

H.J. Mulliner 218
Park Ward 185
James Young 20
Hooper 6
Franay 1
Graber 1

S3 CONTINENTAL[†]

Park Ward 192
H.J. Mulliner 98
James Young 20
Graber 1

[†]ALTHOUGH H.J. MULLINER AND PARK WARD MERGED IN 1961 TO FORM MULLINER PARK WARD, THESE FIGURES RELATE TO THE DIFFERENT DESIGNS OF EACH COMPANY.

THE BENTLEY THAT WENT TO
DINNER AT THE SAVOY

THE Bentley victory at Le Mans in 1927 was the most thrilling and certainly the most 'Bentley' of all its racing triumphs of the Roaring Twenties. Having won in 1924, the victor's laurels eluded the marque in 1925 and 1926, so W.O. Bentley entered not one but three of his cars in 1927.

The race was progressing well for Bentley; as the correspondent of *The Motor* put it, 'there is no doubt that, given reasonable luck, all three Bentleys would have held to the end and covered the greatest distance in the 24 hours.' As dusk fell the 4½-litre Bentley had twice beaten the lap record, and was expected to do so again. Then, when roaring down from Arnage to the White House corner, it found its path blocked by a crashed competitor; in a bid to avoid collision, it wound up in the ditch. Soon it was joined by another Bentley and the crash, which was eventually to claim six cars, also caused crippling damage to the third Bentley, which limped into the pits with a broken headlamp, buckled bodywork, damaged axle and cracked steering arm.

What then occurred was little short of miraculous; patched up with tape, string and with a pocket torch lashed to the windscreen, the remaining Bentley braved a prolonged and torrential downpour of the sort only Le Mans can serve up, to cross the finishing line in first place. It achieved what ought to have been impossible.

Even more significant was that the winning car – Old No. 7, which had competed in the previous year's race – had, according to *The Autocar*, 'filled the interim by serving as a doctor's hack in London.' It was indeed Harley Street consultant Dr J.D. Benjafield and his team-mate 'Sammy' Davis who nursed this valiant Bentley to victory.

At an eleven-course celebratory dinner held in the private banqueting room at the Savoy, hosted by *The Autocar*, the car was an honoured guest: still battered, scarred and filthy from the race, taking a richly deserved place as guest of honour in the middle of a vast horse-shoe shaped table.

THE BENTLEY COCKTAIL

ADAPTED FROM A RECIPE IN *THE SAVOY COCKTAIL BOOK*
BY HARRY CRADDOCK, 1930.

1 1/2 ounces **Calvados or Apple Brandy**
1 1/2 ounces **Dubonnet Rouge**
1 lemon twist for garnish

Stir the Calvados and the Dubonnet
over ice and strain into a chilled
cocktail glass. Add the garnish.

THE WOOLF BARNATO COCKTAIL

ADAPTED FROM A RECIPE CREATED BY
SALIM KHOURY, HEAD BARMAN AT THE AMERICAN BAR
IN THE SAVOY, 2003.

1/3 ounce **vodka**
1/3 ounce **peach schnapps**
1/3 ounce **blue curaçao**
chilled **Champagne**

Pour the vodka, schnapps and curaçao
into a chilled Champagne flute. Top
up with the Champagne.

THE EMBIRICOS BENTLEY

IN 1939, just before the outbreak of World War II, a revolutionary looking Bentley 4½ Litre, styled by the French designer Georges Paulin and built by boutique French coachbuilder Pourtout, tore around the Brooklands motor circuit. It achieved the quite remarkable distance of 114 miles within one hour. Called the Embiricos Bentley, after its plutocratic owner André Embiricos, this was a true supercar, decades before the term was coined.

Flat out on the new autobahns — the arterial roads that criss-crossed Herr Hitler's increasingly big and powerful German Reich — the Embiricos Bentley travelled at speeds in excess of 120mph. To a contemporary motorist such velocity must have seemed more appropriate in the realms of the science fiction of H.G. Wells and Fritz Lang than on the open road. It seemed as though the future had arrived... in the 1930s.

With its mechanical enhancements, streamlined design and lightweight coachwork, the Embiricos Bentley was a phenomenally advanced car. Just how advanced was demonstrated in 1949, a decade after it had stormed round the Brooklands circuit, when the Embiricos Bentley was entered privately at Le Mans and finished sixth. Even more significantly, this car is seen as establishing the pattern upon which Ivan Evernden, Director of Bentley's Experimental Department, would improve in the early 1950s when he was given a cautious go-ahead to develop the R-Type Continental.

AVERAGE SPEEDS OF AND DISTANCES COVERED BY WINNING BENTLEYS AT THE 24-HOUR RACE OF LE MANS

1924	3 Litre	57.5MPH	1,290.59 MILES
1927	3 Litre	61.3MPH	1,472.03 MILES
1928	4½ Litre	69.1MPH	1,658.44 MILES
1929	SPEED SIX	73.6MPH	1,760.97 MILES
1930	SPEED SIX	75.8MPH	1,820.62 MILES
2003	SPEED 8	133.1MPH	3,195.71 MILES

J AMES Bond may be better known as a driver of another well-known British motoring marque, but in the novels of Ian Fleming, he was a Bentley driver. 007's car was introduced in the first of Fleming's spy novels, *Casino Royale*, published in 1953.

> Bond's car was his only personal hobby. One of the last of the 4½-litre Bentleys with the supercharger by Amherst-Villiers, he had bought it almost new in 1933 and had kept it in careful storage through the war. It was still serviced every year and, in London, a former Bentley mechanic, who worked in a garage near Bond's Chelsea flat, tended it with jealous care. Bond drove it hard and well and with an almost sensual pleasure. It was a battleship-grey convertible coupé, which really did convert, and it was capable of touring at ninety with thirty miles an hour in reserve.

This car is damaged in a car chase with Le Chiffre and then is written off while chasing Hugo Drax in the novel *Moonraker*. However, at the end of the novel, Bond takes delivery of another Bentley.

> The 1953 Mark VI had an open touring body. It was battleship grey like the old 4½-litre that had gone to its grave in a Maidstone garage, and the dark blue leather upholstery gave a luxurious hiss as he climbed awkwardly in beside the test driver.

In *Thunderball*, published in 1961, 007 drives a Bentley Continental.

> Bond had the most selfish car in England. It was a Mark II Continental Bentley that some rich idiot had married to a telegraph pole on the Great West Road. Bond had bought the bits for £1,500 and Rolls had straightened the bend in the chassis and fitted new clockwork – the Mark IV engine with 9.5 compression. Then Bond had gone to Mulliners with

£3,000, which was half his total capital, and they had sawn off the old cramped sports salon body and had fitted a trim, rather square convertible two-seater affair, power-operated, with only two large armed bucket seats in black leather. The rest of the blunt end was all knife-edged, rather ugly, boot. The car was painted in rough, not gloss, battleship grey and the upholstery was black morocco. She went like a bird and a bomb and Bond loved her more than all the women at present in his life rolled, if that were feasible, together.

In addition to the bespoke coachwork, there were a couple of other features that set Bentley's Continental apart. 'The twin exhausts – Bond had demanded two-inch pipes; he hadn't liked the old soft flutter of the marque,' and 'the long grey nose topped by a big octagonal silver bolt.'

In the novel *On Her Majesty's Secret Service*, Bond is still driving 'the old Continental Bentley – the 'R' type chassis with the big 6 engine and a 13:40 back axle ratio – that he had now been driving for three years.' However, he had not been able to resist a little light tinkering.

Against the solemn warnings of Rolls-Royce, he had had fitted, by his pet expert at the Headquarters' motor pool, an Arnott supercharger controlled by a magnetic clutch. Rolls-Royce had said the crankshaft bearings wouldn't take the extra load and, when he confessed to them what he had done, they regretfully but firmly withdrew their guarantees and washed their hands of their bastardized child.

ROLLS-ROYCE is not the only marque to have a winged female figure as a mascot on the radiator grille. F. Gordon Crosby, designer of Bentley's winged B logo, also designed an Icarus-style female figure, naked except for a wisp of cloth around her waist and a wing strapped to each arm, which appeared in various catalogues for the Bentley 3 Litre during 1923 and 1924.

THE 1929 SPEED SIX VERSUS
THE 2003 SPEED 8

SPEED SIX		SPEED 8
6.6-litre in line six	ENGINE	4.0-litre V8 turbo
Dunlop crossplies	TYRES	Michelin
11ft (3,353mm)	WHEELBASE	2,735mm
2,000kg-plus	WEIGHT	900kg
Steel ladder frame	CHASSIS	Carbonfibre monocoque
Unstressed	ENGINE MOUNTING	Fully stressed
Beam axle	FRONT SUSPENSION	Pullrod
Leaf	SPRINGS	Twin torsion bars
Twin, friction-type	DAMPERS	Twin
21in x 6¾in	WHEELS	18in x 12½in
Drum	BRAKES	Carbon-carbon discs
	CALIPERS	Six piston
Semi-floating axle	REAR SUSPENSION	Pullrod
Leaf	SPRINGS	Twin torsion bars
Twin, friction-type	DAMPERS	Twin
21in x 6¾in	WHEELS	18in x 13in
Drum	BRAKES	Carbon-carbon discs
	CALIPERS	Six piston
Longitudinal four-speed	GEARBOX	Inboard six-speed, transverse
Single plate	CLUTCH	5½in carbon-carbon
Open	DIFFERENTIAL	VCP
Single, nose-mounted	WATER RADIATORS	Twin, mid-mounted
	AFTERCOOLERS	Twin, mid-mounted
39—44 gallon, rear-mounted	FUEL TANK	90-litre central cell

WOOD VENEERS AVAILABLE FOR
BENTLEY INTERIORS

Bird's eye maple
Burr oak · Burr walnut
Madrona · Olive ash
Dark-stained walnut · Vavona

Each veneer leaf is just 0.6mm thick.

———

It takes 16 leaves to make the 26 main veneered components of a Bentley interior, plus another eight for the waistrails along the tops of the doors.

———

It takes 19 leaves of veneer to create the 17 panels in a two-door Continental GT.

———

Each leaf of veneer can be traced back to the tree it came from.

———

The wood shop uses no bleaching or staining techniques; the rich colour of the veneers is entirely natural.

Burr walnut is the most popular choice of veneer, which can be dark-stained or lacquered to piano black.

———

Endangered wood such as mahogany is not used.

———

You may use wood from your own forest in an Arnage.

———

A fungus in the root ball of the tree produces the distinctive pattern of burr walnut.

———

The most figured veneer comes from the outside of the burl; the deeper inside the burl, the plainer the pattern.

———

The root balls used are usually over eighty years old.

Growers are now developing techniques to improve the quality of the root ball – the secondary use of the tree – as well as the walnuts themselves.

———

Only walnut trees past the best of their nut-producing years are used for veneers; the age range of these trees is typically 60–100 years and the root balls weigh up to 1,500lb.

———

Each tree felled for veneer is replaced with another. For every walnut tree cut down, another three are planted.

———

Bentley is the only coachbuilder to use mirror patterns when applying veneer, placing four successive leaves end to end to make a symmetrical pattern across the fascia – a process known as book matching.

It takes 12–14 days to prepare the wood for an Arnage.

———

The veneers are given five coats of lacquer and three days of curing time before being wax polished by hand.

———

The decorative cross-banding – based on a centuries' old cabinet makers' technique – is still cut by hand in the factory.

———

Rather than the traditional tulipwood, the Continental GT and the Flying Spur are built using aluminium panels as the substrate. Lighter, stronger and thinner than a wooden base, they help Bentley's designers to achieve outstanding space efficiency without losing that inimitable Bentley cockpit ambience.

MOTOR RACING AS A COST-EFFECTIVE PROMOTIONAL TOOL

W.O. Bentley maintained that racing was a cost-effective way of promoting his cars. He believed that once prize money and other income from the company's racing activity had been counted, the amount invested was modest, and he had the figures to back him up:

	RACING	OTHER ADVERTISING
1925	£833	£4,811
1926	£2,412	£4,545
1927	£3,369	£8,613
1928	£2,616	£12,546
1929	£2,487	£14,995

THE Bentley Boys were the motor racing heroes of the Roaring Twenties.

CAPT. WOOLF BARNATO   Considered 'the best driver we ever had' by W.O. Bentley, 'Babe' Barnato exerted almost as powerful an influence on Bentley Motors as its founder. An all-round sportsman, and independently wealthy, Barnato was one of the Bentley Racing Team's outstanding drivers, recording wins at Le Mans in 1928, 1929 and 1930; he remains the only driver to have won on each occasion of entering the race. Barnato's commitment to Bentley Motors extended beyond the racetrack, he provided financial support when the company began to get into difficulties, took over from W.O. as Chairman, and won a seat on the board of Bentley Motors (1931) after Rolls-Royce stepped in to save the marque.

JOHN DUFF   Young and determined, he established a Bentley agency in London, and bought and prepared a 3 Litre in which he set a succession of new speed records at Brooklands. This in itself was excellent publicity for Bentley Motors, but Duff's most lasting achievement came about in 1923 when he called in to the company to request works support for a 24-hour race the French were planning to run at Le Mans. W.O. reluctantly agreed to prepare the car, and to loan Jack Clement as co-driver. The Le Mans course – with its long straights and emphasis on endurance – provided perfect conditions for the Bentley, and the new team performed excellently, finishing fourth despite strong foreign opposition. The following year Duff and Clement recorded the team's first win, defeating many of the leading sports cars of the day.

TIM BIRKIN   Perhaps the most colourful personality in a
team of flamboyant characters, Sir H.R.S. (Tim) Birkin Bart
was an ex-fighter pilot who became the most daring of the
Bentley drivers. Driving in goggles, white drill helmet and
silk scarf, his extrovert personality was always apparent on the
track – and he was often willing to be ruthless with his car to
achieve a result. Having won the 1929 Le Mans race in
partnership with Barnato, he became convinced that even
greater performance could be wrested from the 4½-litre
engine by supercharging it. Despite W.O.'s reservations, a
separate company was formed to produce the 'Birkin
Blowers' which proved to be very fast indeed, though
unreliable. A man who lived life as furiously away from the
racetrack as he did on it, Birkin contracted septicaemia after
burning an arm on the exhaust of his Alfa at the 1933 Tripoli
Grand Prix and died shortly thereafter.

J.D. BENJAFIELD   Known as 'Benjy' to his teammates,
Dr J.D. Benjafield was a Harley Street specialist who knew
little about the mechanical side of a Bentley, but was
nevertheless an excellent driver. Invited to join the team
after entering a Bentley 3 Litre privately at Brooklands in
1923, he drove for Bentley at numerous events, including
Le Mans in 1926, 1927 and 1928.

S.C.H. DAVIS   As Sports Editor of *The Autocar*, 'Sammy' Davis
was already a familiar figure at racing circuits – and a
seasoned driver – when he was invited to partner Benjafield
for Bentley at Le Mans in 1926. Caught out by rain and
failing brakes that year, Davis more than made up for it in
1927, once again driving the famous 3-litre known as

Old No. 7, and gaining the first Bentley win for two years. The win was dramatic: following a multiple pile-up that eliminated all the other Bentleys, Benjafield and Davis drove on with appreciable frontal damage to take the chequered flag for Bentley.

GLEN KIDSTON Described by W.O. as 'a born adventurer: rough, tough, sharp, and as fearless as Birkin,' Glen Kidston was an ex-naval officer who specialised in miraculous escapes. By the time he joined the Bentley team, he was already the sole survivor from an early London–Paris airliner that crashed in fog, and had succeeded in surfacing his submarine after being caught in mud on the seabed. Later, he survived a major crash in the 1929 Isle of Man TT and went on to drive at Le Mans, winning with Barnato in 1930. His luck finally ran out later that year, when his overloaded De Havilland Moth broke up in mid-air whilst touring Africa.

JACK AND CLIVE DUNFEE Unlike some of their teammates, the Dunfee brothers had to work for their living and initially struggled to purchase racing cars. Both had enjoyed successes with other teams before being invited to race with Bentley. Irrepressible in character, Jack quickly became the team joker, while Clive was quieter and more thoughtful. Among other successes, Jack was placed second in a 4½ Litre at Le Mans in 1929, and won the 500 Mile race at Brooklands in 1931. A year later, racing at Brooklands, Clive Dunfee went over the top of the banking and was killed instantly; Jack Dunfee never raced again.

When developing new models, the Crewe works had a fondness for oriental codenames. Exotic locations evoked over the years include:

Tibet
Java
Rangoon
Tonga
Siam
Bengal
Korea
Bali
Panama
Havana
Nepal

4½-LITRE SUPERCHARGED OR 'BLOWER' BENTLEY

W.O. BENTLEY considered that supercharging a Bentley engine was an act of sacrilege, bringing the marque into disrepute. His view, even in later life, was uncompromising.

> To supercharge a Bentley engine was to pervert its design and corrupt its performance.

Nevertheless fifty of these Bentleys were built as road cars and a further five team cars were built and raced, albeit without great success. The supercharger that caused W.O. such distress was an Amherst-Villiers, two-rotor, Roots-type model.

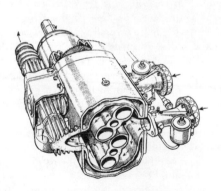

HOW TO SELL A BENTLEY TO A MEMBER
OF THE ROYAL FAMILY

A.F.C. HILSTEAD was the Sales Director of Bentley and this is his account of selling a Bentley to the then Prince George, as published in his 1953 memoir, *Those Bentley Days*.

One evening when I was about to leave the showrooms, a very young man came in and asked if we were still open.

'Tell me some more?' I countered, wondering just a little if I were about to have my leg pulled.

'Well, Prince George is around,' he replied with a cheerful grin.

It is funny the way things happen. I was feeling rather under the weather as sales were not too good, in fact the whole motor trade was finding business extremely slack. That was all very well for the long-established firms who could stand a slump, but for us it was a condition fraught with grave danger. However, the possibility of selling a car to one of the King's sons put a different complexion on the situation. In a few minutes Prince George arrived and I was introduced by his friend who turned out to be a young naval lieutenant. Having gone over the chief points of the polished chassis, I suggested coming upstairs to my office. I took it for granted that I was going to get an order, and so produced a form and began to fill it up. I persuaded the Prince to have a speed model chassis and as he wanted a closed body, pointed out the advantages of a coupé. He was not in the least concerned over the price, and was very definite, over the several accessories required. But when the form was completed, I did wonder if it would be in order to ask a member of the Royal Family to sign it and, this really was a bit ticklish, if I ought to mention the usual 10 per cent deposit. I read over our terms of business without getting any reaction at all, so deciding that the deposit could be waived I handed over the form and offered my pen. The result was 'George' scrawled over the dotted line. Having arranged to give a trial run on the following afternoon,

I drove home in a slightly better frame of mind.

I had no misgivings over the run, for No. 183 was in superb condition and only a wet day could mar the proceedings. It was wet; disgustingly so. Nevertheless, the run took place, also Prince George drove. Some of his methods were certainly original, especially in relation to gear-changing. But he enjoyed his tour of the works, and was utterly oblivious of the several uncouth remarks hurled at his head by an irrational lorry driver in the Edgware Road. It was unfortunate, however, that he left his own car unattended in Hanover Square with two suitcases loose in the dickey. When he returned, the car was still there, but both the cases were missing.

In spite of the wet weather, the abusive lorry driver, the stolen luggage and the... ahem... original gear changes, Prince George liked his Bentley so much that he bought another one. His fondness for the marque has been picked up by his daughter (HM The Queen) and his grandchildren (HRH The Prince of Wales and HRH The Princess Royal).

CAPT. WOOLF BARNATO'S INSTRUCTIONS
FOR THE POST-DOUBLE TWELVE
1930 WIN PARTY

THE race will be run over a number of courses a list of which will be found on your starting places. After having been scrutineered at the Bar, chassis will be parked as the Clerk of the Course directs. As soon as the starting-gun is fired Drivers can let go their clutches and open their throttles wide.

N.B.
1 Always think of the safety of your passenger.
2 How your mechanic looks behind.
3 All spanners, jacks, knives, forks, etc. are the firm's property and must not be taken away.
4 Drivers may only carry one passenger at a time. Passengers may, however, be changed during the Race.
5 Overtaking - A faster car may overtake a slower one, but only if the passenger waves him on.

Before your chassis is parked at its original starting point, each Driver must see that his carburettor is flooded with at least two cocktails. Passengers, mechanics, spare parts and wives are requested to co-operate, and in any event see that this rule is strictly adhered to.

MAP OF THE COURSE
Through the Bar to the Dining-room. After two hours' running in the Dining-room, contestants may try out other chassis in the Ball-room (but only if their own has broken down, seized up or died on them). Refuelling arrangements will by this time be made downstairs. Contestants are specially requested not to sit about in other firm's pits!

BENTLEY PRODUCTION HISTORY
1919 TO 2004

MODEL	YEAR	NO. PRODUCED
CRICKLEWOOD		
3 Litre	1921–1929	1,619
6½ Litre	1926–1929	363
4½ Litre	1927–1931	665
Speed Six	1929–1930	182
4½ Litre Supercharged	1929–1931	55
8 Litre	1930–1931	100
4 Litre	1931	50
DERBY		
3½ Litre	1933–1936	1,191
4¼ Litre	1936–1939	1,241
Mark V	1939–1941	19
CREWE		
Mark VI	1946–1952	5,201
R-Type	1952–1955	2,320
R-Type Continental	1952–1955	208
S1 SWB†	1955–1959	3,072
S1 Continental	1955–1959	431
S1 LWB†	1958–1959	35
S2 SWB†	1959–1962	1,865
S2 Continental	1959–1962	388
S2 LWB†	1960–1962	57
S3 SWB†	1962–1965	1,286
S3 LWB†	1962–1965	32
S3 Continental	1962–1965	312

T1 Two Door	1965–1971	99
T1 D/H'	1965–1971	41
T1 SWB'	1965–1976	1,712
Corniche F/H'	1971–1980	74
Corniche D/H'	1971–1984	88
T2 SWB'	1977–1981	558
T2 LWB'	1977–1981	10
Mulsanne	1980–1987	482
Mulsanne LWB'	1980–1987	47
Mulsanne Turbo	1982–1985	496
Mulsanne Turbo LWB'	1983–1986	24
Eight	1984–1992	1,734
Camargue	1985	1
Limousine	1985–1987	2
Continental	1985–1995	439
Corniche	1982–1985	30
Continental Turbo	1992	3
Turbo R	1985–1997	4,657
Turbo R LWB'	1984–1997	1,508
Turbo RT	1997–1999	252
Mulsanne S	1987–1992	905
Mulsanne S LWB'	1987–1992	61
Mulsanne 'L' Limousine		2
Continental R	1992–2003	1,548
Brooklands	1992–1998	1,429
Brooklands LWB'	1993–1999	191
Brooklands R Mulliner	1997–1998	100
Turbo S	1994–1995	60

BENTLEY PRODUCTION HISTORY
1919 TO 2004

Turbo RT Mulliner	1997–1999	56
Continental S	1994–1995	18
Continental T	1996–2003	349
Continental SC	1997–1999	79
Azure	1995–2003	1,311
Arnage SWB† (4.4-litre)	1998–1999	1,173
Arnage SWB† (6.75-litre)	1999–2002	4,650
Arnage LWB†	2000–	237
Continental GT	2003–	7,003

†LWB = LONG WHEEL BASE; SWB = SHORT WHEEL BASE; D/H = DROPHEAD; F/H = FIXED HEAD

On his combat sortie in a Nieuport during World War I:
'Some basic combat training would have helped in this situation, for I have never left the ground before, fired a shot in anger, nor even seen a Lewis gun, with which I was supposed to defend us from the roaming packs of Fokkers.'

On his work as an aero engine designer:
'From the onset the appalling sense of responsibility hung over me and never left me for the rest of the War: the figure of a pilot killed by engine failure leaning over my shoulder like some ghostly conscience whenever I was at work.'

On being told that the noise from the first Bentley engine was disturbing a seriously ill patient in a nursing home:
'What was the illness of one man? IN HERE the birth of a new engine was taking place.'

On the kind of car he wanted to build:
'a good car, a fast car, the best in its class.'

On the difficulties facing a fledgling car marque:
'To design and build a new motor car in 1919 without substantial capital was like being cast on to a desert island with a penknife and orders to build a house.'

On American cars of the 1920s:
'I am a great admirer of American cars now [1958], but at that time they were really rather terrible.'

On his Sales Director, A.F.C. Hilstead:
'[He] could drive so beautifully that he could have sold a lorry as a limousine to a duchess.'

On the 8 Litre:
'I have always wanted to make a dead silent 100mph car, and I think we have done it.' (A few months later Bentley Motors went into receivership.)

LORE FROM THE SHOPFLOOR

Employees at the Crewe works are often the third generation of a family to work there, so stories are retold and passed down. Here is an example, as recounted by a member of the Bentley workforce in 2005.

We had one customer who came to Crewe to order a car. He was a German officer during the war, but once it was over, he started a successful business. He said, 'I've been to Crewe before, but it was a long time ago when I was a prisoner of war. They kept us in Crewe Hall at the time.' So we arranged for a car to take him back to Crewe Hall, which is a fantastic hotel now. He got quite emotional. They introduced him to the guy that owned the hotel; he was taken up into the roof space where there were names cut into the beams. He told us there used to be a little pub where they were let out to go for a drink. We took him down to the White Lion. I asked, 'You couldn't just go to the pub as you'd try to escape?' 'Oh no,' he replied, 'We wouldn't try to escape. Why would we want to escape from here? It's the most beautiful place. We are German officers and our word is our bond, so we returned at night.' He was quite an elderly gentleman, as you can imagine. I remarked, 'Obviously, you're now very successful.' 'Oh yes,' he said, 'I owe everything to the English because you educated me. All my family were killed in the war so I stayed in England and went to the Coventry area to start a new business. And here I am today, a multi-millionaire coming back to Crewe to buy Bentleys.'

I N 1959, the six-cylinder engine that powered the Bentley
S Series was replaced by a 6230cc V8 engine cast from
aluminium alloy. The new car was designated the Bentley SII.
The same engine appeared in the Bentley SIII. Fitted with new
hydraulic pumps and repositioned spark plugs, the 6230cc V8
appeared in early examples of the Bentley T Series. By 1970,
the engine capacity had been increased to 6750cc. In March
1982, the Mulsanne Turbo was revealed at the Geneva Motor
Show and the turbocharged version of the now 23-year-old V8
boasted an increase in power of at least 50 per cent to 300bhp.
So unstressed was the engine that only minor modifications,
such as an oil cooler and strengthened pistons, were required.

When *The Autocar* magazine tested this car, it raced from
0—60mph in seven seconds, outstripping Daimler's Double
Six, Aston Martin's Lagonda and, most remarkable of all,
the Ferrari 365 GT4. Bearing in mind that the Bentley
Mulsanne Turbo weighed over two tonnes, it can be argued
that, at 23 years old, this V8 was just coming into its own.

By the late 1980s, as it neared its thirtieth birthday, the
engine received another increase in power to 335bhp,
when fuel injection was applied. With the arrival of the
Continental R in the early 1990s, power was boosted to 360bhp
rising by 1994 to 385bhp. It was planned that the engine would
be phased out with the end of the Turbo R series and the mid
to late 1990s saw power output at 407bhp for the limited run
of Turbo and Continental S cars, 400bhp for the Turbo R and
420bhp for the brutish Continental T and the ultra-rare
Turbo RT Mulliner (the ultimate pre-VW Crewe-built four-
door Bentley.)

Just one year short of its fortieth birthday, the V8 disappeared from the new four-door Bentley Arnage, which instead was powered by a 4398cc twin-turbo BMW engine, however it continued to be used for production of the two-door Continental and Azure. But by October 1999, with major re-engineering, the V8 celebrated its fortieth under the bonnet of the Arnage Red Label.

In 2002, the V8 received its most comprehensive engineering makeover and emerged with two smaller turbochargers, instead of one, in the Arnage T, where it was capable of developing 450bhp and dragging this vast four-door car to 60mph in 5.5 seconds and on to an electronically limited top speed of 170mph. According to Brian Gush, Bentley's Engineering Director for Chassis, Powertrain and Motorsport, 'It is the large displacement of each cylinder (just under one litre each), which allows the engine to produce such immense levels of torque at low revs.'

Truly remarkable is the claim of Bentley's Member of the Board for Engineering, Dr Ulrich Eichhorn, that the V8 is not even approaching its limits in terms of bearing and block strength. Bentley V8's power outputs have risen from around 200bhp (150kW) to the 450bhp (336kW) of today's Arnage T and Azure. Now certified to the very latest Euro IV and US LEV I emissions standards, the all-alloy Bentley V8 must clearly be counted as one of the great automotive engines.

LE MANS CIRCUITS FOR THE YEARS
BENTLEY FACTORY TEAMS HAVE RACED

ORIGINALLY conceived as a test of the durability of touring cars of the day, a Bentley was at the very first 24-hour motor race in Le Mans in 1923, when motor sport was in its infancy. It was the only English entry in a field that was otherwise entirely French. However, Bentley quickly came to dominate Le Mans during the Roaring Twenties, racking up win after win after win. The race, run under the aegis of the Automobile Club de l'Ouest, still uses much of the same course, a mixture of track and public road, as it did on that distant May day (these days the race is held in June), but there have been a few changes over the years to make the course safer as cars have become progressively faster and, as happened one year, even airborne. The following diagrams show how the course has changed over the years in which Bentley has competed at Le Mans.

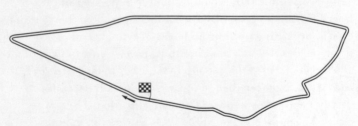

1923–1928 The original course was 10.726 miles long and included a notorious hairpin, Pontlieue, a narrow street crowded with houses. It was popular with spectators as it was potentially dangerous.

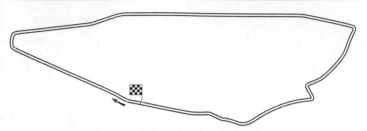

1929–1931 For the 1929 race the Pontlieue hairpin was
removed and replaced by a specially built road, the Rue du
Circuit, which amputated this hazardous hairpin and
shortened the course to 10.153 miles. This incarnation of the
course lasted until 1931.

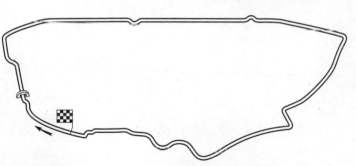

1997–2001 The course on which Bentley returned to Le Mans
in 2001 was considerably shorter than the course on which it
had last driven to victory; the Pontlieue/Rue du Circuit end
of the course had disappeared completely, taking the course
out of the the built up area of Le Mans; thus shortly after the
start, the course followed a right-hand curve under a
footbridge decorated to look like a large Dunlop tyre into the
'Esses' and then a sharp right corner known as Tertre Rouge.

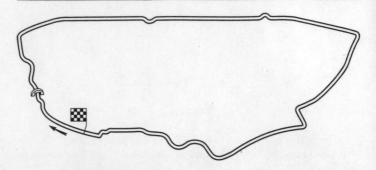

2002— In 2003 Bentley won on a circuit that had changed in 2002, with the straight run from the Dunlop bridge to the Esses being replaced by a series of curves. This current course is 8.48 miles long.

THE ITALIAN BENTLEY THAT
BECAME A ROLLS-ROYCE

IN 1968 Italian coachbuilder Pininfarina, presented a Bentley T1 bodied as a two-door fastback. With its distinctive, aggressive styling and sweeping lower roof edge line that became the line of the upper rear wing, this car was clearly intended to evoke the spirit, speed and style of the R-Type Continental. Although this car was a one-off, it is significant in that it represents an interstitial stage in the story of the two-door Bentley.

Crewe management also saw potential in Pininfarina's design, although not as a Bentley. After a prolonged delay a derivative of the design went into production as the controversial Rolls-Royce Camargue. Although hardly ever specified as a Bentley, it is interesting to note that for road testing, Camargues appeared with the Bentley grille.

1888

Walter Owen Bentley is born on September 16th. He is the youngest of nine children.

Five prostitutes are murdered in the East End of London. Their killer, known as Jack The Ripper, is never brought to justice.

The English Football League is founded. The first season begins on September 8th with twelve member clubs.

1912

W.O. Bentley and his brother, Horace Milner Bentley, open Bentley & Bentley, the UK concession for a French car marque Doriot, Flandrin et Parant (DFP).

The RMS *Titanic* sinks on its maiden voyage from Southampton to New York City.

Pravda, the official newspaper of the Russian Communist Party, is published.

1914

Driving a DFP, W.O. Bentley finishes last in the Tourist Trophy on the Isle of Man.

Franz Ferdinand, Archduke of Austria is assassinated in Sarajevo.

The British Empire enters World War I.

1919

Bentley Motors is founded on January 20th.

The first Bentley engine is tested in New Street Mews in October and later unveiled at the 1919 Olympia Motor Show.

Benito Mussolini founds his Fascist politcal movement in Milan.

The signing of the Treaty of Versailles on June 28th brings a formal end to World War I.

The Weimar Republic is declared in Germany.

1920

New production premises are established at Cricklewood, London, and the first complete Bentley is ready for roadtesting by *The Autocar* magazine. The report by S.C.H. (Sammy) Davis covers two pages and praises the car for its speed, handling, braking and performance.

Sylvia Pankhurst, human rights campaigner and suffragette, is jailed for six months.

Russian Civil War ends with the defeat of Baron Wrangel in the Crimea.

1921

The first Bentley is sold to Noel van Raalte on September 21st.

The Communist Party is formed in China.

Adolf Hitler is elected Chairman of the Nazi Party of Germany.

Benito Mussolini is declared leader of the National Fascist Party of Italy and is elected to parliament.

1922

A Bentley 3 Litre with four-seater body snatches the British Double Twelve Hours record at an average speed of 86.79mph.

The tomb of Tutankhamun is discovered in the Valley of the Kings, Luxor, by Howard Carter after remaining undisturbed since 1337BC.

1923

A Bentley 3 Litre finishes fourth at the 24-hour race at Le Mans.

A former sergeant in the German Army convenes the first congress of the National Socialist Party in Munich.

The Duke of York and Lady Elizabeth Bowes-Lyon marry in Westminster Abbey.

1924

Bentley wins Grand Prix d'Endurance at Le Mans.

Vladimir Lenin, leader of the Russian Revolution, dies aged 54.

Ramsay MacDonald becomes Britain's first Labour Prime Minister.

Adolf Hitler is released from prison on parole, after serving nine months of a five year sentence, and announces that he plans to publish a book.

1925

24-hours world record established at Montlhéry by a Bentley 3 Litre travelling at an average speed of 95mph.

The Bentley 6½ Litre, capable of accommodating heavier and more luxurious coachwork, is launched. It later becomes available as both a standard 6½-litre and the speed model known in the racing world as the Speed Six.

Adolf Hitler publishes his personal manifesto *Mein Kampf*.

Leon Trotsky is removed from power by Joseph Stalin.

1926

Capt. Woolf Barnato rescues Bentley from financial collapse and becomes Chairman of the company.

Princess Elizabeth, later to become Queen Elizabeth II, is born in London.

The General Strike grips Britain.

Claude Monet, the last surviving Impressionist painter, dies.

1927

A Bentley 3 Litre, driven by S.C.H. Davis and Dr J.D. Benjafield, wins the 24-hour race at Le Mans, 212 miles ahead of its nearest rival. F.C. Clement establishes the record lap in a Bentley 4½ Litre.

24-hours Grand Prix de Paris at Montlhéry is won by a Bentley 4½ Litre at an average speed of 52.5mph.

Malcolm Campbell sets the world land speed record of 174.224mph at the wheel of the Bluebird.

Charles Lindbergh flies solo across the Atlantic non-stop in the Spirit of St Louis.

1928

Bentley's 4½-litre engine is launched. 'Tim' Birkin believes that increased performance is to be had by supercharging the engine.

A Bentley 4½ Litre, driven by Capt. Woolf Barnato and Bernard Rubin, wins the 24-hour race at Le Mans.

Leon Trotsky is sent into exile on the Russian-Chinese border.

Amelia Earhart flies across the Atlantic.

Stalin's first Five Year Plan is launched.

1929

24-hours international Class C record at Montlhéry is taken by a Bentley at a speed of 89.57mph.

Bentleys take the first four places at the 24-hour race at Le Mans.

Six Bentleys enter the Irish International Grand Prix and finish in second, third, fourth, fifth, seventh and eighth places.

A Bentley 6½ Litre sets the fastest lap time of 126.09mph at the British Racing Drivers Club 500 Miles Race at Brooklands.

St. Valentine's Day Massacre in Chicago.

Wall Street crashes on Black Thursday.

1930

Bentleys finish first and second at the 24-hour race at Le Mans. The supercharged Bentleys entered by 'Tim' Birkin evince startling performances but do not finish.

The 8-litre Bentley, conceived as direct competition to the Rolls-Royce Phantom, is unveiled.

Amy Johnson becomes the first woman to fly solo from England to Australia.

Joseph Stalin turns Russia over to collective farming.

Uruguay beats Argentina to win the first football World Cup.

1931

Bentley Motors is faced with liquidation. However, Rolls-Royce Ltd steps in, giving the marque a new lease of life as a subsidiary: Bentley Motors (1931) Ltd.

Britain comes off the Gold Standard monetary system.

The construction of the Empire State Building is completed in New York City.

1933

Constructed at Derby and known as 'The Silent Sports Car', the 3½ Litre is the first Bentley manufactured under the direction of Rolls-Royce Ltd. Now employed by Rolls-Royce, W.O. describes it as 'the best car ever to bear his name.' It is designed around the chassis frame of the experimental Rolls-Royce 'Peregrine' project, intended as a smaller, lighter and more economical motor car to keep up sales during The Depression. In practice, it becomes the first example of the winning marriage between the traditional Rolls-Royce attributes of silence, smoothness and refinement and the exceptional performance and sporting handling associated with the Bentley marque.

Adolf Hitler is appointed Chancellor of Germany. One month later, the Reichstag burns down triggering a crackdown by Nazi Storm Troopers.

1936

Bentley offers a 4¼-litre engine and later an overdrive gearbox, as well as a more sophisticated lubrication system.

King George V dies and is succeeded by the snappily dressed Edward VIII.

The Civil War begins in Spain, following a nationalist rebellion led by General Francisco Franco. He succeeds in overthrowing the Republican government to establish a dictatorship.

King Edward VIII abdicates to marry Mrs Wallis Simpson, which leads to the accession of King George VI.

1939

Designed to bring the Bentley in line with Rolls-Royce models, and pre-dating the post-war 'rationalised range', the Mark V is the first Bentley to feature independent front suspension. A Continental version, called the Corniche, is also planned, but the onset of war brings production to an abrupt end. Only 11 of the 19 Mark Vs built are ever completed and fitted with a body.

The Spanish Civil War ends when General Franco conquers Madrid.

Britain declares war on the German Reich.

1946

Fitted with a modified 4¼-litre engine, and with a shortened version of the Rolls-Royce Silver Wraith chassis, the Mark VI is the first motor car to be built entirely at Bentley's Crewe works. It is also the first to be offered with a pressed steel body shell as standard.

Winston Churchill makes his 'Iron Curtain' speech in Fulton, Missouri.

1949

The fabled pre-war Embiricos Bentley is entered privately at Le Mans. It finishes in sixth place.

The Federal Republic of Germany is established.

Britain grants official recognition to Chairman Mao's regime in China.

1950

A 1934 Derby Bentley is entered privately at Le Mans and finishes in eighth place.

Communist North Korea invades the southern half of the country and captures Seoul. The North Koreans are aided by Chinese troops, while the South Koreans are assisted by US forces.

1951

The Embiricos Bentley makes its last appearance at Le Mans and finishes discreetly in twenty-second place.

King George VI and Queen Elizabeth inaugurate the Festival of Britain.

1952

One of the most famous names in the history of the Bentley marque, the Continental, makes its first appearance as a new version of the Mark VI. It features higher gearing, a special low-loss exhaust system and lightweight, streamlined coachwork by H.J. Mulliner. Originally designated simply as the Continental, its name is later changed to the R-Type Continental in order to bring it in line with the R-Type saloon, itself a modified Mark VI with an evolved body. The Continental's ability to run up to 100mph in third gear, with a top speed of just under 120mph, makes it the fastest four-seater car in the world; it soon earns a reputation as the ultimate in high-speed luxury.

King George VI is buried at St. George's Chapel, Windsor. He is succeeded by Queen Elizabeth II.

1955

Rolls-Royce and Bentley now share the same technology. The S Series, the first Bentley to be fully rationalised in this way, differs from its Rolls-Royce equivalent, the Silver Cloud, only in external styling. Only the Continental variant, introduced in the same year and available from specialist coachbuilders in two- and four-door versions, breaks with the styling of the Rolls-Royce range. The S Series remains in production, in different variations, for the same length of time as the Silver Cloud until 1965.

Winston Churchill resigns his post as Prime Minister.

During the 24-hour race of Le Mans, Pierre Levegh's Mercedes-Benz crashes into the grandstand killing over eighty spectators. Levegh is killed outright.

The actor James Dean dies at the wheel of his Porsche Spider aged 24.

1965

The product of several years' intensive development and a dramatically re-designed production line at Crewe, the T Series makes its debut alongside its Rolls-Royce sibling, the Silver Shadow. Engineered by Harry Grylls and styled by John Blatchley, it features all-round independent suspension, four-wheel disc brakes, automatic levelling, full-power braking and air-conditioning. It is also the first Bentley built with a monocoque chassis and body shell.

Sir Winston Churchill is buried at the Palace of Westminster.

The Beatles go to Buckingham Palace to receive their MBEs.

1966

Mulliner Park Ward presents a coachbuilt two-door version of the T Series.

England beats Germany to win the football World Cup at Wembley.

1971

Entering production as the Bentley Corniche, the drophead coupé makes its debut and remains part of the model range until 1984.

Rolls-Royce goes into receivership.

US astronauts go for a spin on the moon.

The United Kingdom and Ireland switch to decimal currency.

1980

Named after the Mulsanne Corner at Le Mans, the Bentley Mulsanne — a version of the Rolls-Royce Silver Spirit — is launched.

Robert Mugabe is elected President of Zimbabwe.

The Iranian Embassy in London comes under seige from terrorists. On the sixth day, SAS troops storm the building in an operation codenamed 'Nimrod'.

1982

A turbocharged version of the Bentley Mulsanne is unveiled at the Geneva Motor Show. Dubbed 'Crewe's Missile', the car is great in a straight line and something of a handful around corners. The model is well received and Bentley sales rise.

John DeLorean's eponymous car company is put into receivership.

Argentine forces surrender to British troops in the Falklands on June 14th, following their invasion of the islands on April 2nd.

Princess Grace of Monaco dies from injuries sustained in a car crash.

1984

The Bentley Eight is launched with a simplified specification, intended to bring Bentley ownership within reach of new, younger customers. Its most striking visual feature is a chrome wire-mesh grille recalling racing Bentleys of the 1920s.

British coal miners begin a twelve-month strike following the National Coal Board's decision to close twenty mines.

President Reagan is returned to the White House for a second term.

1985

The high-performance Turbo R firmly re-establishes the Bentley marque: the R stands for road holding. Effectively a gentleman's club with a 0–60mph time of under seven seconds, it also corners and stops rather well.

Sir Clive Sinclair unveils another vision of British motoring, the electric C5.

Live Aid concerts are held in both London and Philadelphia to raise money for Ethiopian famine relief.

1986

Bentley engines are now fuel-injected.

The US Space Shuttle Challenger breaks up on launch, killing all seven astronauts on board.

Nuclear disaster occurs at Chernobyl.

1991

The two-door Continental R is the star of the Geneva Motor Show.

Operation Desert Storm marks the start of the Gulf War.

1992

The Continental R is put into production. Its turbocharged and intercooled 6¾-litre V8 engine offers 150mph performance.

Bill Clinton is elected President of the USA.

Queen Elizabeth II describes the year as her *Annus Horribilis* following a succession of royal scandals and a devastating fire at Windsor Castle.

1993

The four-door Bentley Brooklands replaces the Eight. From 1996, it features a 300bhp, 6¾-litre, V8, light-pressure turbocharged engine capable of acceleration from 0–60mph in under 8 seconds and a top speed of 140mph.

HM The Queen opens Buckingham Palace to tourists for the first time. Proceeds go towards the cost of restoring Windsor Castle following the fire.

1995

The Bentley Azure, with its distinctive Pininfarina styling, is launched at the Geneva Motor Show. It is the most powerful four-seater convertible in the world.

Fighting ends in Bosnia.

1996

Originally offered in limited production volumes, interest is so great that the muscular Continental T becomes an integral part of the Bentley range. The revised version features a 420bhp engine capable of 0–60mph in 5.7 seconds, a top speed of 170mph and 875Nm of torque – the highest figure recorded for a production motor car.

TRH The Prince and Princess of Wales announce their divorce.

1997

The final year of the Turbo R Series sees the introduction of the Turbo RT. Capable of accelerating to 60mph in under 6 seconds, it enjoys a maximum speed in excess of 150mph.

Bill Clinton begins his second term as US President.

Tony Blair is appointed Prime Minister of the UK.

Hong Kong is returned to Chinese rule.

Diana, Princess of Wales dies following a car crash in Paris.

1998

Bentley is bought by the Volkswagen Group.

The Bentley Arnage is launched at Le Mans. With an engine capacity of 4398cc – the same as the 1928 Le Mans-winning 4½-litre Bentley – the Arnage incorporates new technology throughout. Despite many improvements, the Green Label Arnage does not find favour with marque purists.

President Clinton denies having 'sexual relations' with Monica Lewinsky.

2001

Team Bentley racing programme begins. The Bentley EXP Speed 8 produces more than 600bhp from its 3.6-litre twin-turbocharged engine.

An EXP Speed 8 finishes third at Le Mans.

Terrorist attacks destroy the World Trade Center in New York City.

2002

A Bentley State Limousine is presented to HM The Queen on the occasion of her Golden Jubilee.

HM Queen Elizabeth, The Queen Mother dies at the age of 101.

2003

Bentley Speed 8s, finish third and fourth at the 12-hour race of Sebring in Florida.

Bentley Speed 8, Car No. 7, driven by Rinaldo Capello, Tom Kristensen and Guy Smith wins at Le Mans. Car No. 8, driven by Johnny Herbert, David Brabham and Mark Blundell, finishes second.

President George W. Bush declares an end to major hostilities in Iraq.

2004

Bentley Arnage Limousine (Deep D) enters production as a limited edition of twenty.

Terrorists target rush hour trains in a coordinated attack on Madrid.

An earthquake in the Indian Ocean region causes a devastating tsunami.

2005

Bentley Continental Flying Spur is launched.

Bentley Arnage Drophead Coupé concept is unveiled. It is subsequently confirmed for production as the Azure.

Pope John Paul II dies in Rome.

Terrorists attack the London transport system killing 56 people.

SOME REFINEMENTS CARRIED OUT BY MULLINER, THE SPECIALIST COACHBUILDING ARM OF BENTLEY

Until the 1940s, it was usual for all car makers to supply vehicles with just the rolling chassis and engine; customers then took their car to a coachbuilder for the body and upholstery. This is why so many vintage cars look unique, despite being the same make and model underneath. The firm H.J. Mulliner began as horse-drawn coach builders. They have decades of experience serving customers who specified every minute detail of their car: 86 percent of Arnages go to Mulliner to have some sort of work done. The following is a list of some of the more idiosyncratic requests, and a few that Mulliner was unable to fulfil.

REQUESTS FULFILLED

○ Pipe holders

○ Drawers for chewing gum

○ Safes

○ Fully fitted Sony PlayStations

○ Flat concealed drawers for an antiques dealer to store his paintings

○ Make-up and jewellery trays with specially designed compartments

○ Pink-stained veneers

○ Swivel seats with an automatic raising-and-lowering footrest for a disabled customer

- Raised roof levels for hats/headdresses/crowns

- Talk-in/talk-out microphones on the wing mirrors so there is no need to drop the window glass

- Shotgun cases in the boot

- An Italian customer in the 1990s ordered a Continental R as an ultra-lightweight racing car to look like the Birkin. It had no back seats, a roll cage, a polished aluminium bonnet with a hole for the oil, white circles on the doors for racing numbers (although it was never raced), yellow blades on the fan and quilted seats

- Upholstery matched to the colour of a customer's nail varnish

- Interior trimmed in tweed woven by a customer's own mill

- The rear compartment of an Arnage divided by a curving bird's eye maple console

- Coat of arms embroidered onto each headrest

- Veneer from a customer's own tree

REQUESTS REGRETFULLY DECLINED

○ Alligator hide interior

○ Solid gold radiator shell; failing
that platinum (gold-plated
radiator shells are the norm)

○ Revolving number plates, smoke
and oil screens from the rear of
the car and an electric current
running through the exterior

○ Microwave oven and kettle in
the back of a limousine
(microwaves interfere with the
ABS and steam from a kettle
could damage the veneer)

○ Holder for night-vision
binoculars

○ Quick-release shotgun holders in
the ceiling

○ A lap-dancing pole in the back of
an Arnage (for the production
team of the BBC motoring
programme, *Top Gear*)

O NE-TIME Bentley chairman and three-times Le Mans winner Capt. Woolf Barnato was described by W.O. Bentley as 'the best driver we ever had and the best British driver of his day.' His daughter, Diana Barnato-Walker, became one of the country's greatest-ever pilots. Although forbidden from taking part in active combat she joined the Air Transport Auxiliary during World War II, flying Spitfires to airfields throughout Britain. In 1963 she became the fastest woman in the world, the first female pilot to break the sound barrier.

Accoridng to Brian Gush, Bentley's Director for Powertrain, Chassis and Motorsport, the most important aspect of engineering a car to be capable of almost 200mph is to make sure it can stop again.

In the case of the Continental Flying Spur, a large, luxurious four-seater, the combination of the car's velocity and mass makes the brake system engineer's task far harder than it would be in the case of an equally swift, but lighter single-seater racing car.

Bentley owners with their own private test tracks or airfields can thus take comfort in the massive brake discs fitted to the Continental GT and Continental Flying Spur: at 405mm diameter and 38mm thick, they are the most powerful brakes fitted to any series production car in the world, and will bring the car to a rapid and controlled halt, even from almost 200mph.

LORD SETTRINGTON, BENTLEY'S
ARISTOCRATIC MECHANIC

WHEN my grandfather left Oxford, he became an apprentice at Bentley. At the time, it was very unusual for someone of his background to do such a thing, but he loved it and he later became an engineer and a car designer, so I am sure he learned a lot from his time there and that W.O. was a great influence on him. He was a very unpretentious man. He hated any form of pomposity and whilst lying under a car one day, one of his colleagues who was a mechanic said to him, 'I hear there is some bloody Lord working here,' to which I believe he said, 'Oh, really? I wonder who that could be?'

He never revealed himself, because in those days, as today, snobbery worked both ways and he preferred to be known as plain Freddie March. He then went on to work in the Sales Department of Bentley and the sporting associations of the marque obviously had an effect on him as he went on to race cars, much to the displeasure of my great grandparents. While he was busy winning the Double Twelve at Brooklands in 1934, his parents were having dinner in the Egyptian dining room at Goodwood and the butler brought in the wireless so they could follow the commentary on the race. They asked him to remove it as they refused to acknowledge that their son was pursuing such an occupation as motor racing. Later, of course, he became the ninth Duke of Richmond and Gordon and established the motor-racing circuit at Goodwood.

Charles March on his grandfather, Frederick Charles Gordon-Lennox, the grandest apprentice to work in the British motor industry.

WHEN seen together arranged in order of their appearance, Bentley models display the aesthetic characteristics that have defined the marque over the years, since the name Bentley first enchanted and amazed motorists of the 1920s. The ascent of Bentley has been an interesting one that has taken the brand from the dusty and deadly motor racing circuits of the 1920s, to the garages and car collections of heads of state, billionaires and celebrities from the worlds of entertainment and sport.

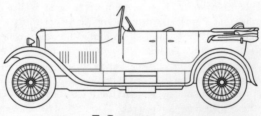

3 LITRE

The one that started it all. In *The Autocar* of January 24th, 1920, the 3 Litre was lauded as a car 'which combines docility in traffic with exceptional speed potentiality on the open road', characteristics which still define a Bentley today. The 3 Litre became a legend, when Duff and Clement recorded their 1924 win at Le Mans in one of these extremely versatile cars.

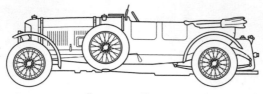

Speed Six

The aim of Bentley's 'Speed' models was to liberate more speed and performance from the standard model. The Speed Six did all that without stressing the engine, therefore maintaining Bentley's reputation for smoothness and reliability. This car was the antithesis to the supercharged 4½ Litre, which W.O. disliked because it perverted his original concept of a Bentley and put undue stress on the engine.

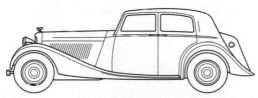

4¼ Litre

The 4¼ Litre was the second Bentley to be produced at Derby under the aegis of Rolls-Royce, making its debut in 1936. It replaced the 3½ Litre as the Bentley of choice due to its superior mid-range performance, giving greater comfort whilst retaining the illusion of sportiness.

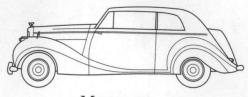

Mark VI

Successor to the Mark V, this was the first post-war Bentley and the first Bentley to be built at Crewe. The corresponding Rolls-Royce model was the Silver Wraith. Significantly the car was also the first Bentley to be offered with standard bodywork by the Pressed Steel Company... unless the customer specified to the contrary.

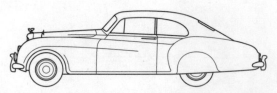

R-Type Continental

The iconic post-war Bentley. During the 1950s this was quite possibly the finest motor car available to humanity, combining speed, performance, luxury, elegance, exclusivity and the evocative Bentley name. Marque purists insist that this was the last true Bentley until the arrival of the Mulsanne Turbo three decades later.

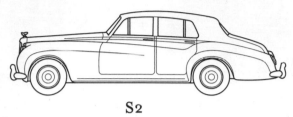

S2

An elegant and understated version of the Rolls-Royce Silver
Cloud II, the Bentley S2 was launched in 1959 and was
powered by the first incarnation of the V8 powerplant that
would characterise Bentleys well into the twenty-first century.

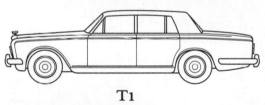

T1

While a perfectly good car, indeed one of the most successful
to issue from Crewe, the T series was nothing more than a
Rolls-Royce Silver Shadow with a Bentley radiator grille and
winged B mascot — even the engine said Rolls-Royce. It was
with the T series that Bentley reached the nadir of its fortunes,
accounting for only a tiny percentage of the combined Rolls-
Royce and Bentley output from Crewe.

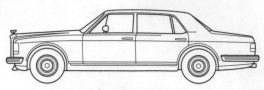

MULSANNE TURBO

By the early 1980s, Bentley's success at Le Mans was over half a century in the past and had little to do with the comfortable saloon cars appearing under the Bentley name. The addition of a turbocharger to the Bentley version of the Rolls-Royce Silver Spirit, heralded the marque's slow return to health. The Mulsanne Turbo was a revelation: supercar performance allied to drawing room comfort.

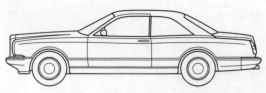

CONTINENTAL R

A gorgeous car – the ultimate late twentieth-century gentleman's express – the Continental R and its derivatives redefined grand luxe two-door motoring. It was recognised as a classic the moment it was launched.

ARNAGE

Like the Mulsanne, the Arnage evoked the glories of the
Le Mans era. It was the first Bentley since the late 1950s not to
be powered by the trusted V8. However, popular demand
ensured that before long the Arnage was powered by the
traditional unit and sales accelerated accordingly. The Arnage
has given birth to the forthcoming Azure, which is the latest in
Bentley's long heritage of elegant open-top cars.

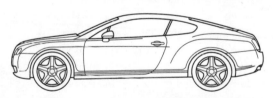

CONTINENTAL GT

The first new-generation Bentley. The Continental GT became
the It-car of the early twenty-first century in much the same
way that Bentleys captured the imagination in the Roaring
Twenties — sleek, purposeful and capable of transporting its
occupants at 200mph in contemporary Bentley luxury. Out of
the GT was born the Flying Spur, a four-door car capable of
almost the same levels of performance.

BENTLEY SPECIALS

A BENTLEY Special is the name given to a car based on Bentley, but tinkered with or otherwise adjusted to deviate substantially from production models. Bentley Specials are usually built for speed.

THE BARNATO-HASSAN SPECIAL — built in 1933 using the 6½-litre engine from Old No. 1 and a mixture of other Bentley parts, the engine was replaced by an 8-litre unit in 1934; a lap time of 142.6mph was recorded in this car. It was rebuilt in 1936 and achieved a fastest lap time of 143.11mph. After the war, it was rebuilt again.

THE PACEY-HASSAN — built in 1935 using a 4½-litre engine and when this engine broke in 1936, it was replaced by a supercharged 3-litre engine. It was rebuilt as a road car after the war and then returned to its original body style by a subsequent owner.

O N MAY 17th, 1929, *The Autocar* printed details of the latest royal Bentley under the headline 'Prince George's New Car'.

Very imposed and dignified is the four-door enclosed limousine on a Bentley Speed Six Chassis which J. Gurney Nutting & Co. Ltd., have just completed for H.R.H Prince George. The Body is of Weymann construction and is finished in black fabric with chromium-plated radiator, lamps, and small external fittings. The interior is upholstered in furniture hide with a very soft and supple surface, and the window winders and other interior fittings are exquisitely carried out in Florentine bronze, this metal also being used for the instrument board. The interior woodwork is of ebony with a pewter inlay, and Splintex glass is used throughout.

Incidentally, this is the second Weymann body which J. Gurney Nutting & Co. Ltd., have had the honour of building for Prince George, and the car is extremely comfortable and yet capable of a high performance. A D-shaped partition is fitted at the back of the front seats, and the large centre panel is provided with a winder. The main seat has a folding centre arm rest and large well-padded rests at the sides. Companions of ebony and pewter inlay are let into the rear quarters. Particularly striking are the lines of the car, with its cycle type wings and steps in place of running boards. A large luggage trunk is fitted at the rear, but does not obstruct the filler of the petrol tank.

LEATHERS AVAILABLE FOR BENTLEY INTERIORS

Standard hide colours currently available for an Arnage are:

COLOUR	BENTLEY NAME	COLOUR	BENTLEY NAME
BLACK	*Beluga*	GREY	*Cinder*
	Portofino		*Porpoise*
			Portland
BLUE	*French Navy*		*Slate*
	Nautic		*Stratos*
	Peacock		
		BROWN	*Autumn*
RED	*Burgundy*		*Burnt Oak*
	Fireglow		*Cognac*
	Redwood		*Cotswold*
			Ochre
GREEN	*Laurel*		*Saddle*
	Loxley		
	Savannah	CREAM	*Linen*
	Spruce		*Magnolia*
			Oatmeal
			Saffron

- The Bentley hide shop can match almost any colour.

- Hides are sourced from herds in Northern Europe; chosen for the area's lack of barbed-wire fences and warble flies.

- A full set of leather for an interior is selected and cut at the same time, so that there is as little variation in texture as possible.

- Bentley achieves 55–65 percent hide usage – the best in the industry.

- Steering wheels are double-stitched by hand; the process is far too complicated for a machine. It takes 15 hours' work to create one steering wheel.

- A full set of trim consists of 400 separate pieces.

- Each piece is marked with the chassis number of the car for which it is intended.

- Every machinist who creates a finished piece of upholstery signs it on the back with his or her initials.

- Each hide is minutely inspected for imperfections; even something as slight as an insect bite will cause the hide to be rejected.

- It takes 10-14 hides to trim the inside of a Continental GT, 12 for a Flying Spur and a minimum of 17 for an Arnage.

- Unusual requests for seat coverings include ostrich, deerskin, and cavalry twill and tweed.

- The trimming of each Bentley Continental GT uses 135m of thread; the equivalent of 28 GTs back-to back, 1.3 football pitches or the height of the London Eye.

THE factory now has a 'shake rig' to test for squeaks and rattles, which is configured to replicate, exactly, a test drive of 50 miles round Crewe. No longer do they need to shut a mechanic in the boot to listen out for noises, but there is still no better mechanism for tracking down noise than the human ear, so a mechanic is still required to sit inside each car on the 'shake rig'.

HM THE QUEEN'S GOLDEN JUBILEE STATE LIMOUSINE BY BENTLEY

DESIGN started in January 2000.

TESTING of the prototype started March 31st, 2002.

BUILDING of the second car started April 1st, 2002.

FINISHED vehicle presented May 29th, 2002.

HM THE QUEEN has previously had Rolls-Royce motor cars, most of which had been modified for ceremonial duties. Her first Rolls-Royce was a 1947 Phantom IV presented by the RAF on the occasion of her marriage to HRH The Prince Philip.

THE BENTLEY was designed for her, taking her seated position as the starting point.

IT IS lower than her Phantom VI State Limousine, but has more interior height.

IT HAS 800mm wheels and a specially developed suspension system to cope with the added weight of the car.

THE INTERIOR is upholstered using grey West of England cloth to the rear and dark blue leather to the front.

ALL HM THE QUEEN required as features were a clock, a radio, a cd player, powerful air-conditioning and two 'occasional' seats.

AFTER a gap of 73 years, Le Mans in 2003 saw the return of Team Bentley to the top steps of the podium to record the marque's sixth victory. The drivers of Team Bentley 7 and 8 for that emotional homecoming thus became the newest Bentley Boys.

CAR NO. 7

TOM KRISTENSEN was born on July 7th, 1967. The Dane has won Le Mans in 1997, 2000, 2001, 2002, 2003 (with Bentley), 2004 and 2005, eclipsing the record of the great Jackie Ickx and becoming the most successful Le Mans racing driver of all time.

RINALDO CAPELLO also known as Dindo, was reckoned by many to be the quickest sportscar driver on the grid in 2003, having recorded pole position in both the previous two years, 2001 and 2002. He won at Sebring in 2001 and 2002, and currently has two Le Mans victories to his credit.

GUY SMITH was Le Mans Rookie of the year in 1999, and the sole remaining member of the 2001 Team Bentley line-up that recorded a remarkable third-place on Bentley's return to Le Mans. He was described as quick, gutsy and with an innate sympathy for the feel of a car.

CAR NO. 8

MARK BLUNDELL started in 61 Formula One Grands Prix, and his career has encompassed motorcross racing, F1 and Indycar. The winner at Le Mans in 1992, he and his team-mates claimed second place for Team Bentley in 2003. He is now a well-known TV motorsport commentator.

DAVID BRABHAM is a British-born Aussie who has raced in Formula One, Formula 3000 and Formula 3 before becoming one of the world's leading sportscar racers in the American Le Mans Series and at Le Mans itself.

JOHNNY HERBERT is a veteran of over 160 Grands Prix, with three Grand Prix victories to his name. He is also one of the most popular of British racing drivers and fought his way back courageously from an accident in 1988 that left him with severe injuries to his feet and ankles. He won Le Mans in 1991... for Mazda.

BENTLEY & CO. — a Bond Street jewellers founded in 1934 at No. 65 New Bond Street. Now Bentley & Co. is part of Bentley & Skinner, jewellers by Royal Appointment to HM The Queen and HRH The Prince of Wales.

ARTHUR BENTLEY — an American political scientist who was particularly influential between World War I and World War II. According to *The Penguin Dictionary of Politics*, his main contribution was the bold and daring assertion 'that all political systems really consisted of a number of separate groups competing with one another for influence over policy'. He also pointed out that the sun rises in the east and sets in the west.

DEREK BENTLEY — British teenager who was hanged on January 28th, 1953 for murder and pardoned posthumously in 1998.

NATHANIEL BENTLEY — eighteenth-century dandy, aka the 'Beau of Leadenhall' aka 'Dirty Dick', as in later life he adopted slovenly habits and became a byword for squalor.

SIR RICHARD BENTLEY — classical scholar of the seventeenth and eighteenth centuries who exercised virtually despotic power as master of Trinity College Cambridge from 1700 until his death in 1742. According to *The Oxford Dictionary of National Biography*, 'among his numerous contributions to classical scholarship may be mentioned his discovery and restoration of the "digamma" to certain words in the Homeric poems'; a fact for which the world remains grateful to this day.

WES BENTLEY — American comic actor.

THE 8-LITRE ENGINE

W.O. BENTLEY'S last engine design for the cars that bore his name was, in many eyes, the best. The 8 Litre was more expensive than the Rolls-Royce Phantom and judged by many to be a far better car, in terms of comfort, luxury and speed. On December 5th, 1930, *The Autocar* recorded a ½ mile terminal speed of 101.12mph. Between then and the outbreak of World War II, only one other car recorded a faster speed. Coming as it did at the beginning of the Depression, the 8 Litre is also seen as the design that contributed to Bentley going into receivership.

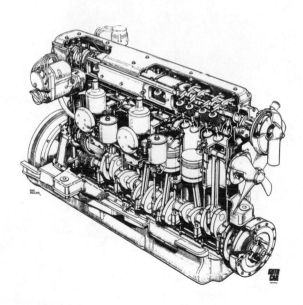

THE famous criss-cross pattern of the mesh grille was not an original feature of the radiator; it was developed by John Duff as a stone guard, to protect the honeycomb-shaped cooling elements of the radiator from stones thrown up during racing.

PROTECTIVE CLOTHING WORN BY BENTLEY
MOTOR RACING DRIVERS

B ACK in the Twenties, racing drivers were less well protected against the rigours of their sport and any special items of clothing were worn for superstitious rather than protective reasons. For instance, Birkin said he would not like to drive without wearing his blue and white scarf or a special crash helmet with his old St. Christopher in it. However, he did admit to one piece of protective clothing.

> I also wear a sort of glorified tummy band, which is invaluable; it keeps my inside together when I am being jolted up and down for hours on end, and in an accident, might prevent the steering wheel from driving into my lungs.

This somewhat devil-may-care attitude, which contributed both to the appeal and deaths of many early racing drivers, is in contrast to the sartorial preparations made by Team Bentley drivers in the 2003 24-hour race of Le Mans, when even the drivers' boots were stitched together using flame-resistant thread.

PAINT COLOUR MATCHING

WHEN Jack Barclay ordered a new Bentley in 1936, he picked a flower from his garden and asked for the paint colour to be matched. Despite the wide choice available in Bentley's range of paint finishes and hide colours, some owners settle for nothing less than an exact match to some prized object or favourite shade. During a visit to Crewe, while deliberating the shade of blue he wanted, a customer spotted the exact hue he was after on the tie of a Bentley employee. Scissors were found and the said piece of neckwear was cropped to provide a sample for a precise colour match. To date Bentley's paint shop has been asked to match a club tie, a pair of cufflinks, a shade of nail varnish, a classic pre-war racing car and even, on one occasion, a sequin from an evening gown. They have yet to be defeated by a request.

BENTLEY ADVERTISEMENTS

ALTHOUGH W.O. Bentley felt that racing was a more cost-effective way of promoting his motor cars, advertisements for the marque have appeared peripatetically since his day. Some of them are true masterpieces of the copywriter's art, demonstrating the contempt for restraint and addiction to hyperbole for which the advertising profession is famed.

> In the Beginning Bentley Motors set out to build the world's finest sporting car, and they succeeded admirably. When they turned their attention to luxury and comfort they were equally successful. A test run on one of the 6½-litre cars is always, to me, slightly embarrassing, as there is literally nothing that one can find to criticize... It is silence and flexibility personified, while the riding comfort is just about as good as it is possible to get. Every part of the car seems to enter into a sort of silent conspiracy to perfection and to blend its duties into one harmonious whole.

Country Life encomium quoted in an advertisement for the marque circa 1930.

Bentley The World's Finest Car

Clearly unassailed by self doubt, advertisement for the 8 Litre

100mph without noise

The extravagant claims of the advertisements, compensated for the understatement of the car, advertisement for the 8 Litre

Other countries have built very fast touring cars, to which all credit be given. But it is none the less pleasant to know that Britain now boasts a still faster car which is so unobtrusive, so refined, so docile and so all-round silent that it actually made its debut as a super-town carriage!

Advertisement for the 8 Litre, appealing to the patriotic spirit of the British car buyer

Proved on Road and Track – Behind every Bentley is a series of racing triumphs without precedent in the annals of motoring. No other car has been so thoroughly proved in international events on road and track. The extensive and valuable experience gained in these strenuous tests is utilized to the full in the production of all Bentley models, resulting in an ever increasing degree of reliability and safety.

Just in case you were in any doubt as to W.O. Bentley's commitment to racing, advertisement for the marque circa 1930.

Bentley The Silent Sports Car

The strapline that came to define an era of Bentley history, advertisement for the 3½ and 4½ Litre

The 3½-litre Bentley is the most amazing proposition which it has ever fallen to my lot to handle.

Sir Malcolm Campbell in an effusive mood quoted in an advertisement for the 3½ Litre.

Take a Bentley into partnership

An advertisement for the S Series, extolling its business virtues... but only for partners in the firm.

The Bentley Continental

With coachwork by Park Ward

The outstanding performance of the Bentley Continental is still further enhanced by greater power from the engine, with larger carburetors, larger inlet valves and compression ratio of 8:1. The special lightweight body owes much to aircraft methods of construction and the front seats have been "anatomically" designed to give better grip when cornering at speed. There is a Drophead Coupé version of the same car.

Blinding the buyer with aerodynamics and anatomics, an advertisement for the Bentley Continental, October 1956

The Bentley Continental R.

Two cars for the price of four.

The Continental R became a classic motor car the moment it swept onto highways and byways, reintroducing connoisseurs to the real meaning of 'gran turismo': a motor car that provides the epitome of comfort over long distances and, when requested, performs like a whole stable of thoroughbreds.

At the merest press of a button, the gears are held for longer, the suspension responds to the change in pace and the Continental R is transformed from a luxurious tourer into something altogether more sporting.

You will find no single other car will ever capture the essence of the Continental R.

No matter how many you buy.

The world may have been in recession but Crewe was still peddling the virtues of conspicuous consumption, advertisement for the Continental R, October 1992

BENTLEY BADGE COLOURS

CRICKLEWOOD BENTLEYS

BLUE   3-litre standard models; 6½-litre models; 8-litre models; (all standard models apart from 4½-litre)

RED   3-litre 'Speed' models

GREEN   3-litre 'Supersports' models – the '100mph 3-litre'; 'Speed Six' 6-litre models

BLACK   4½-litre models; 'Blower' and normally aspirated models

DERBY BENTLEYS

From 1931 onwards, all badges were black.

CREWE BENTLEYS

RED   Mulsanne Turbo; Turbo R; Continental R; Arnage R

BLACK   Continental T; Arnage T; Continental GT; Continental Flying Spur; Azure (2006)

BLUE   Azure

YELLOW   Continental R 1995, a special model, The Giallo Quaranta (meaning Yellow Forty, to reflect Italian dealer Carlo Talamo's favourite colour and age)

GREEN   1996 anniversary (all badges were green for one year's production), 1998 Arnage 4½-litre twin-turbocharged

BRIAN GUSH, Engineering Director for Chassis, Powertrain and Motorsport, Bentley Motors explains:

> Torque is the force that changes a steady state of motion; if you are trundling along at a certain speed and want to go faster, it is the torque that you feel changing the rate of motion. Torque differs from power (as expressed in brake horsepower) in that torque is the force that changes the rate motion, while power is the force that maintains it. In a Bentley, torque is very much in the foreground of the driving experience; and is particularly appreciated at low revs, giving an impression of effortlessness in the engine, creating a very British gentle rumble as opposed to the wail of an Italian V12.

> The torque curve is arranged with the torque (expressed in Newton metres or lb/ft) placed on the vertical axis shown relative to rpm along the horizontal axis. The Bentley torque curve is characterised by rising to its maximum at low rpm (around 2,000) and staying constant at that maximum value up until maximum rpm.

Effortless torque remains an essential characteristic of any Bentley engine, and a more reliable guide to 'real-world' performance than horsepower figures alone. In the case of the 6-litre Bentley W12 engine, a mountainous 650 Newton metres of torque is available from as little as 1,600rpm, and remains at this level right through to 6,000rpm.

ENGINE PERFORMANCE CURVE
6-LITRE W12 ENGINE

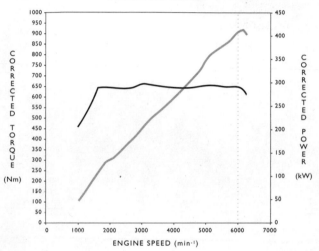

A DEFINITION of torque, taken from *The Shorter Oxford English Dictionary*

TORQUE (*from Latin torquere, to twist*) physics and mechanics, a twisting or rotating force, esp. in a mechanism; the movement of a system of forces producing rotation.

Not to be confused with

TORC a necklace of twisted metal particularly favoured by the Ancient Celts.

THOSE wishing to combine the tactile pleasures of a Bentley cockpit with the gustatory delights of a good dinner can now do so at Anton Mosimann's private dining club in Belgravia. The Bentley room, which features a stunning collection of photography depicting Bentley's sporting heritage, seats fourteen around a table inspired by the fine wood inlays of a Bentley dashboard. Each of the dining chairs is crafted in the finest green leather, its design modelled on the seat of a 1920s Cricklewood era racing Bentley. Each seat also carries a brass plaque inscribed with the name of a famous 'Bentley Boy' — or girl.

THE EVOLUTION OF THE BENTLEY DASHBOARD

OVER the years the amount and nature of information to be relayed to the driver has been changed, likewise the controls and their functions have altered the geography of the dashboard over the years. In addition to the basic equipment of rev counter, speedometer, odometer, etc., the twenty-first century Bentley driver uses dashboard instrumentation to check on the temperature, watch television and alter the suspension... while enjoying a back massage delivered by the ergonomically correct seating.

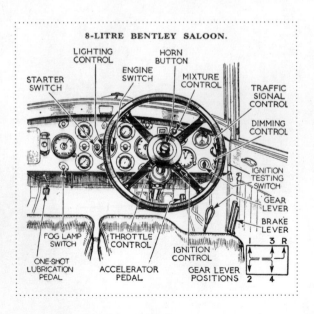

8-LITRE BENTLEY SALOON.

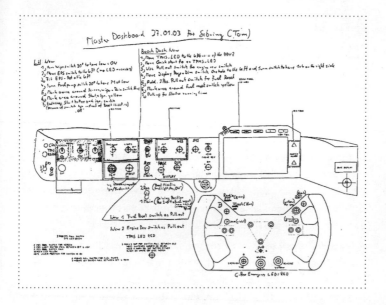

ABOVE Such is the complexity of the 2003 Speed 8, even experienced racing drivers need a crib sheet to navigate their way through the various switches controlling the ignition, engine revs, fuel resets, fuel pumps and, of course, wipers. This is Tom Kristensen's sketch of his car's cockpit.

LEFT In contrast to the Speed 8, the cabin of the 1930 Bentley 8 Litre exudes a stately simplicity.

Another Blue Train Exploit

**CAPT. WOOLF BARNATO REACHES LONDON
BEFORE BLUE TRAIN GETS TO CALAIS**

An unpremeditated, but thoroughly successful, achievement was put up by Captain Woolf Barnato, driving his standard Speed Six Bentley saloon, on Thursday and Friday, March 13th and 14th [1930]. During the course of a discussion before the start, Captain Barnato was wondering whether it was possible, with ordinary comfort, to reach London by a quicker method than using the Blue Train. It was therefore decided to leave Cannes at the same time as the famous express, with the intention of being back in London by half past three the following afternoon.

A feature of the drive was that the start was made from Cannes instead of from Saint Raphael, which made it necessary to cross the Esterel mountains – a slow piece of road. On the other hand, the French section of the run was ended at Boulogne instead of at Calais. On Thursday evening Captain Woolf Barnato and Mr T.A. Bourne, who were on holiday on the Riviera, waited in the Carlton Bar at Cannes until they were told that Blue Train had started.

They then got calmly into their Bentley saloon and set off for London. They arranged by telephone for Esso filling stations to remain open at Lyons and Auxerre, and, leaving Cannes at exactly 6 p.m. on Thursday, they reached Boulogne at exactly 10.30 a.m. on Friday. They then embarked on the 11.35 boat, reached Folkestone soon after 1 o'clock, and reached the R.A.C. in

Pall Mall at 3.30 p.m. The average speed across France worked out at 43.43mph, and although the weather was good as far as Lyons, except for about 25 minutes' driving in fog, torrential rain and a blustering wind set in so that they had wet roads for almost the entire journey.

They made no attempt to put up high speeds, and although the Bentley was naturally capable of doing a lot more then 75mph they never exceeded this speed even on the most favourable roads.

As a matter of interest the schedule time for the Blue Train to leave Cannes is 5.26 p.m., and it is due at Calais at 3.45 p.m. the following day; passengers travelling by this train are scheduled to reach Victoria at 7.15 p.m., so that, including the Channel crossing, Captain Barnato actually reached London 3¾ hours sooner than he would have done if he had travelled by the Blue Train.

From Russia with Love (1963)	4 ½ Litre
The Junkman (1982)	Mark VI
The Dead Zone (1983)	S1
Sabrina (1995)	Turbo R
The X-files: The Movie (1998)	Continental Turbo
Wild Things (1998)	Continental
Gone in Sixty Seconds (1999)	1999 Arnage, 1999 Azure and 1964 Continental
The Thomas Crown Affair (1999)	Arnage
Charlie's Angels (2000)	Azure
The Family Man (2000)	S3 Continental
Les insaisissables (2000)	Mulsanne
Exit Wounds (2001)	Arnage
Ocean's Eleven (2001)	Arnage
28 Days Later (2002)	Continental
Simone (2002)	S3 Continental
2 Fast 2 Furious (2003)	Continental R 8
Michel Vaillant (2003)	EXP Speed 8
Agent Cody Banks II: Destination London (2004)	1951 R-Type Continental
Albert est méchant (2004)	Brooklands
Laws of Attraction (2004)	S2
The Life and Death of Peter Sellers (2004)	R-Type Continental
The Punisher (2004)	Arnage
San Antonio (2004)	Corniche
She Hate Me (2004)	Arnage
Surviving Christmas (2004)	Arnage R
The Wedding Date (2005)	Mark VI

THE PRICE PAID BY ROLLS-ROYCE
FOR BENTLEY IN 1931

THE price paid by Rolls-Royce for Bentley in 1931 after the latter had gone into liquidation: **£125,275.**

BENTLEYS THAT NEVER MADE IT INTO PRODUCTION

BLIZZARD a feasibility study conducted in 1950 into creating a Bentley sports car capable of competing with other models on the market in terms of speed and acceleration. The project was shelved when its performance failed to exceed that of the Jaguar XK 120 with which it was being compared.

JAVA a 1994 concept car based upon the BMW 5 Series platform and developed by Bentley and BMW engineers, which was overtaken by the sale of Bentley to Volkswagen.

JUNIOR BENTLEY a four-cylinder Bentley designed by John Blatchley in 1946.

PROJECT 90 COUPÉ a 1985 concept car, known by insiders as the Black Rat.

PROJECT HUNAUDIÈRES a track car for the road presented in 1999, powered by a W16 engine capable of developing 623bhp and 760Nm or 561 lb/ft of torque at 4,000rpm.

SCALDED CAT a car so hair-raising that it frightened the board of Rolls-Royce into scrapping the model.

SUN a prototype with a $4\frac{1}{2}$-litre six-cylinder engine was abandoned when W.O. Bentley decided an extra 2 litres were required following a race with the new Rolls-Royce Phantom in France in 1924. Although the Bentley did not lose the impromptu road race with the Rolls-Royce, it was not fast enough for his taste.

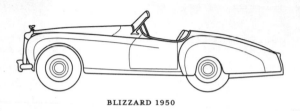

BLIZZARD 1950

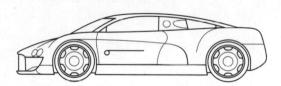

PROJECT HUNAUDIÈRES 1999

BENTLEY CHAIRMEN

BENTLEY MOTORS
MANAGING DIRECTORS

W.O. Bentley

Capt. Woolf Barnato

ROLLS-ROYCE LTD CHAIRMEN	ROLLS-ROYCE LTD MANAGING DIRECTORS
1931–35 Lord Wargrave	1931–44 A.F. Sidgreaves
1936–43 Lord Herbert Scott	1945–50 E.W. Hives
1944–50 Eric Smith	1951–53 Lord Hives &
1951–55 Lord Hives	A.G. Elliot (joint)
1956–67 Lord Kindersley	1954–67 F. Llewellyn-Smith
1968–71 Sir Dennis Pearson	1968–71 G. Fawn

ROLLS-ROYCE MOTOR HOLDINGS LTD
CHAIRMEN

1973–79 I.J. Fraser

ROLLS-ROYCE MOTOR HOLDINGS LTD
MANAGING DIRECTORS

1973–79 David Plastow

CHIEF EXECUTIVES

1971–80 David Plastow

1980–82 George Fenn

1982–88 Richard Perry

1988–94 Peter Ward

1994–97 Chris Woodwark

1997–99 Graham Morris

1999–2001 A.D. (Tony) Gott

BENTLEY MOTORS LTD
CHAIRMAN

2001–present Dr F.J. Paefgen

CREWE has been the home of Bentley since 1946, but the factory where today's Arnage, Continental GT, Continental Flying Spur and Azure are crafted was originally built in 1938 to make the famous Rolls-Royce Merlin V12 aero engine, which powered the Spitfire, the Hurricane, the Lancaster and the P51 Mustang. At its peak in 1943 the factory employed 10,000 people, and morale was maintained by visits from the Halle orchestra, Gracie Fields and even the King and Queen. To disguise the factory from the air the roofs of the buildings were painted to resemble fields and farmland. Despite these imaginative precautions, the factory was bombed in 1940 with the loss of sixteen lives. Nonetheless, by 1945 over 15,000 aero engines had been produced at Crewe.

COLOUR OPTIONS FOR
THE BENTLEY ARNAGE

The joy of owning a Bentley is that it need not be like any other. One of the most obvious ways for an owner to set his stamp on a car is through the colour of the bodywork, matching or clashing with the interior trim, or paired in two-tone combinations.

PAINT COLOURS (41)

Alpine
Anthracite
Antique Gold
Arctica
Barnato Green
Beluga
Black Sapphire
Black Velvet
Brewster
Bronze
Burgundy
Burnt Oak
Chestnut
Coral
Cypress
Dark Sapphire
Diamond Black
Fountain Blue
Glacier White
Grey Violet
Iridium

Laurel Green
Magnolia
Meteor
Midnight Emerald
Moonbeam
Moroccan Blue
Neptune
Oxford Blue
Peacock Blue
Royal Ebony
St James
Silverlake
Silver Storm
Silver Tempest
Spruce
Storm Grey
Sunset
Tungsten
Umbrian Red
Verdant

Main hide colours (27)

Autumn	Oatmeal
Beluga	Ochre
Burgundy	Peacock
Burnt Oak	Porpoise
Cinder	Portland
Cognac	Portofino
Cotswold	Redwood
Fireglow	Saddle
French Navy	Saffron
Laurel	Slate
Linen	Stratos
Loxley	Savannah
Magnolia	Spruce
Nautic	

Carpet colours (14)

Autumn	Fireglow
Black	French Navy
Cirrus	Granite
Cognac	Laurel
Conifer	Nautic
Dark Blue	Oatmeal
Dark Mocha	Redwood

COLOUR OPTIONS FOR THE BENTLEY ARNAGE

LAMBSWOOL RUG COLOURS (12)

Autumn

Black

Cirrus

Conifer

Dark Blue

Fireglow

French Navy

Granite

Mocha

Nautic

Oatmeal

Redwood

SEATBELT COLOURS (6)

Black

Bronze

Pampas

Pewter

Pimento

Spruce

VENEER TYPES (8)

Bird's Eye Maple

Burr Oak

Burr Walnut

Dark Stained Walnut

Madrona

Olive Ash

Piano Black

Vavona

INLAY (4)

Oak cross-banding	Walnut cross-banding
Oak straight-grain boxwood	Walnut straight-grain boxwood

FINE LINES (32)

Autumn	Nautic Blue
Beluga	Oatmeal
Burgundy	Ochre
Burnt Oak	Peacock
Cinder	Porcelain White
Cognac	Porpoise
Cotswold	Portofino Blue
Eucalyptus	Redwood
Fawnesse	Saddle
Fireglow	Saffron
French Navy	Savannah
Gold	Signal Red
Laurel	Silver
Linen	Slate
Loxley	Spruce
Magnolia	Stratos

THE GOLDEN BOOK

In 1969, to mark the fiftieth anniversary of the foundation of Bentley Motors, a book was created by F. Sangorski and G. Sutcliffe Ltd of Soho. This book was sent around the world to be signed by those who had an association with the early days of the marque. In 1986, the same book was sent around the world to be signed by various members of the Bentley Drivers' Club to mark the fiftieth anniversary of the organisation. The book travelled over 60,000 miles, took 31 flights and journeyed in 73 Bentleys. It covered more than 8,000 miles by Bentley in countries including: England, South Africa, Zimbabwe, India, Australia, New Zealand, Canada, USA, Switzerland, Germany, Holland, Sweden and Norway.

BEFORE he became associated with four-wheeled motor vehicles, W.O. Bentley was a keen biker. In 1906, W.O. purchased a belt-driven, 3hp Quadrant, 'the first mechanically propelled vehicle any Bentley had ever owned.' His brothers, H.M. and A.W., soon followed suit buying another Quadrant and Triumph respectively. W.O. and A.W. then entered the London to Edinburgh Trial in 1906 and each won a gold medal, even though W.O. was hampered by a dead ignition and a flat tyre. W.O.'s next motorcycle was a 3½hp machine constructed by Bellinger. By 1908 he was astride a 5hp Rex, winning gold medals in two long-distance trials from London to Plymouth and back and to Land's End and back. He entered the 1909 Tourist Trophy (TT), on a different Rex, a 3½ Speed Model but skidded out of the race without even completing the first lap. Later that year, he entered a one-hour race at Brooklands. It was at this point that he began to show his engineering genius as some modifications he had made to improve reliability and lubrication for racing were later incorporated by Rex in their standard production models. Later, in 1909, he won a gold medal at the Six-Days Trial, which took place over the Welsh hills. In 1910, he entered the TT with an Indian, and managed a first lap time of 19 minutes and 27 seconds before being put out of the race by tyre failure. However, the following day he logged the fastest time up the Snaefall hill climb. His last competitive ride was back at Brooklands in the One-Hour TT. However, he took to two wheels again during World War II, using a Francis Barnett 98cc model to commute between his home and the Lagonda factory, where he was working.

THE PROBLEMS IN MAKING A CAR TRAVEL
AT 200MPH

ONE might think that if a 100bhp car can achieve 100mph, a 200bhp car of the same size ought to be able to achieve 200mph. Unfortunately not: the laws of physics dictate that the power required to increase the speed of a car rises exponentially. In the case of the Bentley Continental GT, an engine producing 300bhp – a respectable enough figure – would be capable of accelerating it to a maximum speed of 155mph. But pushing the Continental GT through a wall of air to a top speed of almost 200mph requires almost double that amount of power; hence the 552bhp output of the 6.0 litre twin-turbocharged W12 engine.

Furthermore, the science of aerodynamics is an exacting one, and making a car both stable and composed at speeds approaching 200mph is no easy task. When designing the 552bhp Continental Flying Spur, Bentley's engineering team eschewed the simple solution of a boot-mounted spoiler as they felt it would spoil the purity of the car's lines. Instead, at speeds above 155mph the luxury four-door saloon's air suspension lowers the nose by 10mm and the rear end by 25mm. A diffuser, hidden behind a grille within an aperture in the rear bumper, is the foundation of the aerodynamic performance of the car. It reduces rear-end lift at high velocities and makes the car feel stable, rather than nervous, as speed increases towards the double-ton.

It would be entirely possible for Bentley to give the Continental GT or Continental Flying Spur even higher top speeds by designing bodyshells with a lower Cd, or coefficient of drag. Unfortunately the brakes, engine and the air conditioning would not function reliably for very long in such a machine. The reason? Cooling. Airflow management is a specialised discipline all its own; as well as ensuring that the car remains stable at high speeds, the major challenge in airflow management is that of channelling cooling air into the radiator, intercooler, brakes and air conditioning system at all speeds and in external temperatures of 50°C or more... and then extracting it again. Cooling slows the car — but also keeps it going.

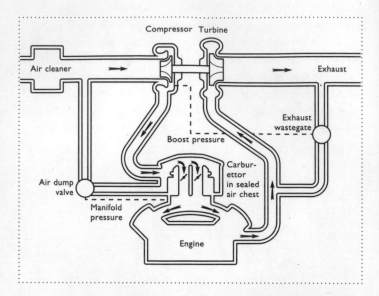

PUT SIMPLY, a turbocharger increases the amount of fuel and air pumped into cylinder by using exhaust gases, which would otherwise have been expelled through the tailpipe, to drive a pump using a turbine type system. Turbocharging is more fuel-efficient than supercharging, where the engine power is used to drive a pump fulfilling the purpose.

THE STORY OF THE BENTLEY 'JEWEL' FUEL FILLER CAP

N O JOB is too big for Mulliner, but nor is any detail too small. Typical is the story of the filler cap. One American customer felt that the filler cap on his Arnage was, well, a little pedestrian for such a great car. Even though it was kept out of sight, concealed beneath a flap in the bodywork he wanted someone to do something about it.

This owner was working on the sound principle that every part of his Bentley, with which he came into contact, should be a joy to see, to touch and to operate. His filler cap was not and he asked Mulliner to make a rather more elegant bespoke item to keep his petrol from spilling out of the tank. This is a rather more complex process than one might imagine; what may be a simple filler cap to some, is a vital component in the fuel integrity system to those responsible for vehicle safety legislation.

Mulliner pointed out, politely of course, that they would be more than happy to accommodate this customer's request, but that there might be some, ahem, fairly heavy 'development costs'. No matter, said the customer, and Mulliner received a blank cheque to devise the filler cap.

Pretty soon, other Mulliner customers got to hear of this gleaming new filler cap that made refuelling a pleasure, rather than a chore. The customer for whom it had been made was approached to see if he minded it being made available to fellow Bentley drivers.

As the Bentley Mulliner Options Portfolio shows, the Bentley 'Jewel' Fuel Filler Cap is now available to all Mulliner customers. In thanks, Mulliner sent the original customer a cheque for the development costs, less the list price of the filler cap. The customer was so pleased that he did not bank the cheque, but framed it instead.

TESTING TIMES

B EFORE any Bentley is released for production it will have covered over a million miles in testing, including extremes of temperature from the Arctic Circle to Death Valley, Arizona, as well as being driven to its limits at internationally recognised venues such as the Nürburgring, Nardo and the Grossglockner mountain pass. From over 50°C to below -30°C, not only must the interior climate control maintain a constant set temperature, but all other components, including locks, hinges and gas struts for the boot and bonnet must operate perfectly.

During cold-weather testing, a Bentley is driven close behind a specially designed sled, which creates a snowstorm in miniature. Called Snow Ingestion Testing, this tests the ability of the radiator, engine and underbody to cope with a massive volume of blizzard-force snow. At the opposite extreme, to ensure that a Bentley's hand-selected leather upholstery and fine wood veneers do not bleach in strong sunlight, test samples are left in the mouth of an extinct volcano, one of the hottest and most destructive of all environments.

Putting a 552bhp Bentley through its paces is a job for a skilled driver, and all Bentley's accredited testers have to pass an exacting examination of their driving skills before being allowed to take the wheel at venues such as Germany's Nordschleife track at the Nürburgring. As an extra precaution, the factory at Crewe has a seat rig that can be rotated upside down so that drivers can practice extricating themselves from a Bentley that has rolled onto its roof. To date, this particular skill has not been called upon on location at either road or track.

Back in the early days of Bentley, the company's chief test driver was W.O. Bentley himself, who used to take off on long, solo drives to Scotland and back, or down into France and over the Alps. 'At the wheel I could not only beat out from the car any possible troubles,' he noted in his autobiography, *My Life and My Cars*, 'but I also found it the most fruitful place to think out the answers to them.' With due respect to W.O. Bentley, the principles today are the same, but the methodology and the size of the engineering team at Crewe makes the current generation of Bentleys the most thoroughly tested of any in the marque's history.

Most knowledgeable motorists know the difference between a 'straight' and a 'V' engine, but the 'W' configuration of Bentley's turbocharged 12-cylinder engine may puzzle some. In essence, the W consists of two narrow-angle V6 crankcases sharing a common crankshaft (itself an object of some wonder and beauty to the technical aficionado). The advantage of this layout is that it is extremely compact, keeping weight close to the centre of the car and also allowing more space ahead of the front axle for the all-important crumple zone.

The W12 engines that power the Bentley Continental GT and Bentley Continental Flying Spur are assembled by hand. The engine's bare crankcase and an entire 'kit' of parts for each engine is mounted on an Automatic Guided Vehicle (AGV), which is self-powered and equipped with laser-guidance tracking that follows defined black lines painted on the floor. The AGV visits each of the 16 assembly workstations in strict sequence, and remains at each for exactly 17 minutes. It thus takes 4½ hours to build a Bentley engine to the point where it is ready for testing. Each engine is run for at least 30 minutes, with 10 percent of engine production being run for up to 48 hours under full power.

AFTER Bentley's victory against all odds in the 1927 Le Mans, Lord Iliffe, proprietor of *The Autocar*, proposed a toast at the Savoy hotel victory dinner: 'To a lady who should be here' — upon which the double-doors opened and the victorious Bentley 3 Litre made its entrance.

With such an honourable tradition, it was only fitting that the sixth Bentley Le Mans victory in 2003 should be celebrated in the same way. To accommodate the winning Speed 8, the entire revolving door of the Savoy had to be removed, and then, to access the ballroom, the car had to be tipped through 45 degrees.

After dinner, an impromptu contest was held to see who could climb aboard the Speed 8 cockpit in the shortest possible time: naturally, team drivers weren't allowed to enter. Derek Bell, five-times winner of Le Mans, posted a creditable time. However, the evening belonged to Capt. Woolf Barnato's daughter, Diana Barnato-Walker, who at the age of 85 kicked off her shoes and wriggled into the car to tumultuous applause.

Dr Franz-Josef Paefgen made an historic toast of his own: 'W.O.' The entire room stood in appreciation of the quiet engineer, whose name and spirit still permeates everything Bentley makes and does.

ACKNOWLEDGEMENTS

THANKS for contributions and assistance to Sophie Robinson, Nick Swallow, Mark Tennant, Richard Charlesworth, Brian Gush, The Bentley Drivers' Club and The Vintage Sports Car Club.